A DIFFERENT KIND OF ETHNOGRAPHY

A DIFFERENT KIND OF ETHNOGRAPHY

Imaginative Practices and Creative Methodologies

Edited by

Denielle Elliott and Dara Culhane

UNIVERSITY OF TORONTO PRESS

Library and Archives Canada Cataloguing in Publication
A different kind of ethnography : imaginative practices and creative methodologies / edited by Denielle Elliott and Dara Culhane.

Includes bibliographical references and index.
Issued in print and electronic formats.
ISBN 978-1-4426-3661-3 (paperback).—ISBN 978-1-4426-3662-0 (hardback).—ISBN 978-1-4426-3663-7 (pdf).—ISBN 978-1-4426-3664-4 (html).

1. Ethnology—Methodology. I. Culhane, Dara, 1950–, author, editor II. Elliott, Denielle, 1970–, author, editor

GN345.D53 2016   305.8001   C2016-901956-X
                                                                  C2016-901957-8

We welcome comments and suggestions regarding any aspect of our publications—please feel free to contact us at news@utphighereducation.com or visit our Internet site at www.utppublishing.com.

North America
5201 Dufferin Street
North York, Ontario, Canada, M3H 5T8

2250 Military Road
Tonawanda, New York, USA, 14150

ORDERS PHONE: 1-800-565-9523
ORDERS FAX: 1-800-221-9985
ORDERS E-MAIL: utpbooks@utpress.utoronto.ca

UK, Ireland, and continental Europe
NBN International
Estover Road, Plymouth, PL6 7PY, UK
ORDERS PHONE: 44 (0) 1752 202301

ORDERS FAX: 44 (0) 1752 202333
ORDERS E-MAIL: enquiries@nbninternational.com

Every effort has been made to contact copyright holders; in the event of an error or omission, please notify the publisher.

The University of Toronto Press acknowledges the financial support for its publishing activities of the Government of Canada through the Canada Book Fund.

Printed in the United States of America.

Poem on p. 27 reprinted from Adrie Kusserow, "Thirty-One, Anthropologist, No Gods Left" in *Hunting Down the Monk*. Copyright © 2002 by Adrie Kusserow. Reprinted with the permission of The Permissions Company, Inc., on behalf of BOA Editions, LTD., www.boaeditions.org; p. 29, "Ghetto Teachers' Apology," by permission of Whitepoint Press LLC.; and pp. 29-30, Renato Rosaldo, "Coloured Marshmallows," in The Day of Shelly's Death, p. 88. Copyright 2014 Duke University Press. All rights reserved. Republished by permission of the copyright holder. www.dukeupress.edu.

CONTENTS

IMAGES

PREFACE

This edited collection is a result of the collaborative imaginings of the five contributors who are co-curators at the Centre for Imaginative Ethnography, a research collective focusing on experimental and emergent ethnographic methodologies that integrate and fuse creative arts, digital media, and sensory ethnography, and where new ethnographic writing is encouraged in teaching, theory, and practice. Inspired by creative, artistic, and literary forms, we were drawn together by our shared interests in creating spaces where we could disrupt, question, and contest the usual anthropology, and create new installations, performances, stories, ethnographies, and theories that bridge our commitment to socially relevant, timely, rigorous scholarship about the worlds we live and work in.

We celebrate the productive tensions that emerge from collusions of art, performance, ethnography, and theory, and between activists, artists, scholars, and our interlocutors as sites of possibility and transformation. We encourage our members to engage in conversations that explore the visual, textual, urban, spatial, poetic, political, performative, improvised, embodied, reflexive, kinetic, ethnographic, emergent, creative, and imaginative in our scholarship and pedagogical practices.

At the Centre for Imaginative Ethnography website, you will find resources on sonic ethnography and the politics of sound, graphic novels and animation in anthropology, moving images and film, literary ethnography and creative non-fiction, and experiments in theatre and performance—along with details about our members. We encourage you to visit the website at www.imaginativeethngoraphy.org, and explore, share, and contribute.

Denielle Elliott
Dara Culhane

CHAPTER 1

IMAGINING: AN INTRODUCTION

Dara Culhane

IMAGE 1.1: Piano, Strathcona Community Gardens, Vancouver, Canada.

Credit: Dara Culhane, 2014.

> *Reality leaves a lot to the imagination.*
> *—John Lennon*

Sana is daydreaming in class again. She is trying to focus on what her professor is saying but there is some force transporting her to some other place, some other time. She hears him describing their term project . . .

"Your essays must be 14 pages long. Please ensure they are typed, or word-processed, double-spaced, in Times New Roman 12-point font, with 2.54 centimeter margins on the top, bottom, and the sides. Is this clear? Are you reading along with your assignment sheet? Please highlight these formatting instructions because . . ."

Sana wonders, Are university classes meant to sap or encourage her creativity? Her imagination? How important it is that she know how to format papers with 2.54 centimeter margins? And why Times New Roman? Could he pick a font that is any less interesting? It is her least favorite.

She doesn't want to conform, to write within the margins, or make her work look standard. She wants to explore the deep, dark crevices of her imagination, to find the glowing, shimmering light of hope and creativity sparkling there.

Sana would rather draw her term paper. She imagines drawing a paper for her economic anthropology class, depicting Microsoft as a hairy, fat monster that eats everyone and then burps out a pile of vomit, and then the Gates Foundation rising up in the steam . . . she'd draw in charcoal, she thinks. Or maybe she could dance her term project? Ah, yes, she'd perform the market domination of Apple and its reliance on violence and dangerous mining practices in the Congo with a mash-up of music—Seun Kuti's IMF song, Pink Floyd's "When the Tigers Broke Free," and a little Green Day. She'll demonstrate with physical movement how mining steals lives, rapes bodies, and destroys the environment. Or perhaps she might write a poem—an angry, poetic rap rant that rails against the economic maneuverings of Big Oil.

Sana imagines a different university, a different anthropology, one with space for her imagination and creativity to emerge, develop, and be nurtured—in tune with the critical, scholarly lessons that she is passionate about. She yearns for an anthropology that can speak to sounds, tastes, smells, and sensations, one that can describe her hopes and her fears, her dreams and her nightmares.

She imagines . . .

What Is Ethnography?

We take imaginative and creative ethnography as points of departure— an invitation to live differently, to animate spaces, classrooms, and stages, to listen carefully to the lives of others, to use humor and imagination to write, picture, and perform the world alive.

—Centre for Imaginative Ethnography, "Welcome to CIE," 2016 (www.imaginativeethnography.org)

What is ethnography? Whether you are new to this field, or, like the authors whose work you will encounter here, you already call yourself an ethnographer, you have likely been confronted by a multitude of possible answers to this question. In *A Different Kind of Ethnography: Imaginative Practices and Creative Methodologies* you will read about work designed to foster an approach to ethnographic methodology of the kind that our opening character Sana longs for.

The five authors whose work you will read about here are co-curators at the Centre for Imaginative Ethnography (CIE) (www.imaginativeethnography. org), a transnational research collective whose members include scholars, artists, artist/scholars, activists, and practitioners around the world. The CIE offers a space for exploring emergent ethnographic methodologies such as those that you will read about in this book. The work we offer you here interweaves experimental ethnographic writing (Elliott, Chapter 2), sensory ethnographies (Culhane, Chapter 3), sound studies and digital media (Boudreault-Fournier, Chapter 4), walking and image-making (Moretti, Chapter 5), and storytelling and performance (Kazubowski-Houston, Chapter 6). The five contributors to this book currently teach at Canadian universities, and our geopolitical research sites span Canada, Cuba, Ireland, Italy, Kenya, and Poland.

Imaginative Practices and Creative Methodologies are vital to our ethnographic research, our teaching, and our work at the CIE.

We consider imagination and creativity as practices that we all engage in every day, that shape and are shaped by social relations, politics, and cultural formations that infuse lived experience. In each chapter of this book you will find participatory exercises that invite you to write in multiple genres, to pay attention to embodied multisensory experience, to create images with pencil and paper and with camera, to make music, and to engage in storytelling and performance as you conceptualize, design, conduct, and communicate ethnographic research. These exercises offer you a set of experiences with which to think ethnography critically and reflexively through practice, and to consider what differences it may make to act with ethical and political awareness around your own and others' engagements with ethnography.

Most contemporary ethnographers would agree that the focus of ethnographic research continues to be what anthropologist Tim Ingold describes as "entangled relationships" among humans, nonhumans, and natural, social, and virtual environments. "The environment," Ingold writes, "comprises not the surroundings of the organism but a zone of entanglement" (2008, 1797). The methodology you will read about here flows from theoretical approaches that assume that ethnographic knowledge emerges not through detached observation but through conversations and exchanges of many kinds among people interacting in diverse zones of entanglement. This is what we mean when we refer to ethnography as a methodology of inquiry into "collaborative" or "co-creative" knowledge making.

The question, What do ethnographers do? animates this book, and the chapters demonstrate how answers are shaped not only by training in university and college courses in research methods but also importantly by the peoples and places where ethnographers work, by the objectives of particular research projects, and by the backgrounds and interests of specific ethnographers. Rather than step-by-step "how to do ethnography" instructions, this book offers you examples to read about, exercises to do, and questions to think with, which we hope will inspire you to imagine how *you* might practice ethnography imaginatively, creatively, and rigorously.

But what do ethnographers *do*? The venerable anthropologist Clifford Geertz (1998) famously wrote that ethnographers engage in "deep hanging out" with people as they and we go about living our lives. Ethnographers join others working, playing, caring for kith and kin. Perhaps we help out. We eat meals together; we attend ceremonies, social and sports events, parties, protests, academic conferences, professional association meetings, religious services, concerts, and much more. We listen to people telling stories about themselves, their families, their neighbors, and other researchers. We share stories of our own. These, of course, are activities that most everyone carries out in one way or another during the course of everyday life, and that researchers in many disciplines as well as anthropology also engage in. Quetzil Castañeda (2006, 78) writes that what differentiates ethnographers are the questions and ideas we carry "in the backs of our minds." These questions and ideas come through multiple avenues: They are shaped by our own embodied, lived experiences and our entanglements with cultural beliefs and practices, histories and social/political relations, and academic theories and debates we learn when we are educated and trained in particular disciplines, interdisciplines, and transdisciplines.

Taking as given that "knowledge is power," the political potential of ethnographic methodology lies in deepening our understandings of the micro-political, relational processes involved in knowledge co-creation (Biehl 2013). Investigating how these embodied processes move through zones of entanglement offers us insights into power at work and leads us to understand methodological questions as epistemological ones: How do we know what we know? What knowledge and whose knowledge counts, and why?

Like the complex and ever-changing ways of life we study, our ethnographic research practices too are entangled with historical/political/cultural processes and thus shift and change over time and across space. We turn now to a brief introduction setting out how *A Different Kind of Ethnography* develops from critical traditions in anthropology and engages with contemporary debates about ethnographic methodology, where it has come from, where it might be going, and why it matters.

A Short History of the Present

In other words, one cannot reduce understanding to a method, because the researcher and object of inquiry are always historically situated and historically related. . . . The fusion at the center of understanding means that we must see knowledge production as a flexible, creatively, historically influenced process.

—Allaine Cerwonka (2007, 23)

The ideas about ethnographic research that we anthropologists carry in the backs of our minds are shaped in part by our critical understandings of the theorizing about peoples and cultures and how to study human relations that disciplinary ancestors worked on through many generations. The most transformational critiques that shape contemporary anthropology were initiated by spokespeople for Indigenous decolonization movements in settler colonies like Canada, the United States of America, Australia, and Aotearoa/New Zealand, and national liberation struggles in Europe's former colonies in Asia and Africa that emerged following World War II and strengthened during the 1960s and 1970s (Biolsi 1997; Said 1989, 1993). These movements challenged anthropology's complicity with colonial and neocolonial governments, and demanded rights to self-representation and control over research as integral to political struggles for self-determination (Simpson 2014). Feminist (Behar and Gordon 1991), queer (Lewin and Leap 2001), post-colonial (Mahmood 2011), and environmental scholarship (Bodley 2008) aligned with activist movements and also advanced critiques of anthropology, ethnographic research practices, and representation throughout the closing decades of the twentieth century. These continue

IMAGE 1.2: Etienne—La Conversacion (The conversation).
Escultura Donada ala oficiana del historiador de la cuidad de la Habana por Vittario Perrotta, 25 Mayo 2012, Havana. (Plaza San Francisco de Assisi, Havana, Cuba. Donated by Vittorio Perrotta to the City of Havana, 25 May 2012. This represents the need for dialogue in contemporary society.)

Credit: Dara Culhane, 2013.

to invigorate contemporary anthropology. A critical tradition of work by relatively marginalized twentieth-century anthropologists like Zora Neale Hurston, Ella Deloria, Ruth Landes, and many others constitutes an alternative canonical lineage through which many contemporary ethnographers now trace their disciplinary ancestry.

The 1986 publication of *Writing Culture: The Poetics and Politics of Ethnography*, co-edited by historian James Clifford and anthropologist George Marcus, is often pointed to as marking the beginning of the contemporary critique and reconstruction of anthropology. The authors of *Writing Culture* argue persuasively against a historical anthropology modeled on the natural sciences and informed by positivist social theories that had dominated the discipline since the late nineteenth century. They critique conventional publications that emulate the monologic, authoritative style of a scientific report written by a presumably neutral and detached observer. Contrary to the positivist model, the contributors to *Writing Culture* argue, anthropologists and people they work with engage in a dialogic process of knowledge co-creation and circulation. Texts created by ethnographers therefore emerge from conversations and exchanges among researchers and collaborators who are active agents engaged in studying their own and other's cultures, histories, and epistemologies. This process is significantly shaped by the relationship between researcher and research participant or collaborator, which is, of course, entangled in diverse and complex histories and politics. Ethnographies, Clifford and Marcus argue, are more productively and appropriately written and read as literary works employing rhetoric, writing styles, and authorial strategies that share more in common with novels than with laboratory reports.

The critiques of institutional structures and disciplinary canons that have occupied contemporary anthropological thinking have focused on relationships between ethnographers and research participants, on the politics of representation and the limits of conventional textual forms, and on questions about the public relevance of anthropology. Research participants now demand ethical engagement with scholars in research projects. Many expect equitable distribution of the benefits of research and the right to refuse participation they deem potentially harmful or irrelevant to the best interests of their constituencies. This in turn has brought forth demands for inclusion and recognition of the analytic value of embodied, affective, and experiential knowledge, and critical, subaltern analyses. The world in which we live and work is changing, and so too must the ways we live and work.

Reflecting on shifts that have taken place in the 25 years since the publication of *Writing Culture*, George Marcus noted a proliferation of experimental texts and ethnographic films; increases in collaborative projects involving anthropologists, scientists, humanities scholars, artists, artist/scholars, and activists;

and an exponential growth in development and use of digital technologies. He writes that "the most lively contemporary legacy of the 1980s *Writing Culture* critiques now lie[s] outside, or beyond, conventional texts but, rather, in the forms that are integral to fieldwork itself" (Marcus 2012, 47). Indeed, in their introduction to *Theory Can Be More Than It Used to Be*—a companion volume to *Fieldwork Is Not What It Used to Be* (Faubion and Marcus 2009)—Boyer and Marcus (2015, 3) explain that "both works are methodological reflections, soundings of how the classic norms and objects of anthropological research and training have become unraveled and reordered in the late 20th and early 21st centuries." They go on to argue that paying analytic attention to methodology as processes of knowledge co-creation facilitates epistemological critique. That is, researching how we come to know what we know clears paths for ethnographers and collaborators to take often-marginalized forms of embodied, affective, imaginative, and creative knowledge seriously, and in this way to challenge and transform social theory "from the bottom up" by intervening at the site of its production.

Also flourishing now are interdisciplinary collaborations among anthropologists, artists, and artist/scholars animated by shared critiques of their respective disciplinary histories, by excitement about new possibilities that such collaborations invite, and by visions of possible futures (Schneider and Wright 2006, 2013). Roger Sansi writes of artists who conceptualize their work as social practice and who share questions and commitments with many contemporary anthropologists as follows: "Stepping outside the gallery space, these artists have proposed explicitly social and political forms of work. The aim of their projects is not just to enact social relations, but to intervene in actually existing contexts—to have a social and political effect" (2015, 13). At the same time, anthropologists, following the work of disciplinary predecessors like writer Amitav Ghosh (1994), filmmaker Jean Rouch (Stoller 1992), performance theorist Victor Turner (Turner and Schechner 1988), and others, have been taking up creative writing, photography and filmmaking, sound and music, visual arts, performance, exhibition, and installation as expressive and communicative forms more attuned to the complexities of representing ethnographic research materials and fieldwork experience. While anthropologists have conventionally considered the artistic *products* created by research subjects as objects of study, many contemporary anthropologists and artists are turning their attention to creative methodologies, to articulating ethnography and artistic practices in the *process* of research, and to ethnographic knowledge co-creation. In this new and emerging work, artistic practices and ethnographic methodology are integrated into research design, practice, analysis, and development of products for communication with diverse publics. In his analysis of research-based work by three contemporary Lebanese artists, anthropologist Mark Westmoreland argues that the "generative possibilities enabled by crossing disciplinary boundaries between art and anthropology" (2013, 723) are to be found in shared commitments to inquiries into sensory, embodied, affective experience that critiques "both what constitutes knowledge and how it is acquired" (738).

Recognition and support of innovative work at intersections of anthropology, ethnography, and art is evidenced by the journal *Anthropology and Humanism*'s long-standing annual ethnographic fiction and poetry contests, and new developments such as Ethnographic Terminalia. Since 2009, this has been an installation at the American Anthropology Association annual meetings that describes its objectives as follows: "No longer content to theorize the ends of the discipline and possibilities of new media, new locations, or new methods of asking old questions, Ethnographic Terminalia is working to develop generative ethnographies that do not subordinate the sensorium to the expository and theoretical text or monograph" (Ethnographic Terminalia, n.d.). Ethnographic Terminalia has created a lively space for anthropologists to showcase the creative possibilities of social research that escapes convention and pushes boundaries by playing with new media, graphics, the acoustic, material art forms, and photography (see Brodine et al. 2011).

In the chapter by Alexandrine Boudreault-Fournier ("Recording and Editing," this volume) we see how such conventional methods can be transformed and strengthened with new sound and image technologies, and how what we know is related to our modes of attention. When we record sounds or images, we develop a fine awareness of the sonic and visual worlds that surround us; this implies that we become more fully aware of the sounds and sights that we often take for granted. The "cinematic imagination" forces us to imagine the world visually and cinematically, one that plays out when filmmakers record images and sounds as well as when they edit a film; it is also engaged when people watch or listen to audiovisual or sonic media. Collaborators working with Cristina Moretti ("Walking," this volume) narrate walking tours they create to explore questions about their relationship to the city of Milan, Italy, where they live. Randia, an elderly Roma woman, and Magdalena Kazubowski-Houston ("Performing," this volume) together create a performance script that interweaves Randia's life stories with a fictional fairy tale.

Dialogue, collaboration, ethical engagement, imagination, and creativity have become keywords in late twentieth- and early twenty-first-century anthropology and ethnography. Contemporary ethnography demands ethical accountability and collaboration in relationships between researchers and research subjects, and political responsibility to communities where research is carried out. Indigenous and feminist anthropologists, in particular, are actively recreating conventional theory and methodology (Smith 1999; Davis and Craven 2016). Environmental anthropology has emerged as significant in recent decades as anthropologists document and reflect on the impact of climate change, oil-based capitalism, and environmental disasters like Hurricane Katrina and the Fukushima Daiichi nuclear disaster (Kottak 1999), and a vibrant field of critical public anthropology demonstrates why ethnography matters in the contemporary world (Fassin 2013; Morris 2015).

Thinking about ethnography in these terms leads us to pay critical attention to relationships between and among researchers and research participants, and this in turn has sharpened our intellectual and political commitments to reflexivity and to analyzing relations of power and questioning how these shape ethnographic research. It has become common and expected practice for researchers to take an analytic account of similarities and differences between themselves and research participants, such as those structured by race, class, gender, and sexuality, and to ask how these political positions may shape research relationships. Dara Culhane's chapter explores how sensory ethnography demands new practices of "sensory embodied reflexivity" in order to take theoretical/methodological account of how ethnographers and collaborators are embodied, feeling, imaginative, and creative beings (Katzman 2015; Green and Hopwood 2015). Magdalena Kazubowski-Houston recounts her process of writing a fairy tale, "Iridescence," based on her research relationship with Randia, an elderly Roma woman in Poland, and her work to adapt it for the stage. By detailing how she thought through the challenges of this process, Kazubowski-Houston allows the reader to accompany her through the ups and downs of their co-creative journey. One comes face-to-face with the surprises, promises, risks, and difficulties that she and her collaborator encountered in trying to convey their stories and in negotiating the tensions between ethnography and fiction, research and art, anthropologist and interlocutor.

A Different Kind of Ethnography

"Ethnography," in our usage, refers to a methodology: embodied, affective, relational processes of knowledge co-creation, and re-circulation that develop from, elaborate and enrich, and challenge and subvert conventional ethnographic methods such as participant observation and observant participation, interviewing, documentary and archival research.
—Centre for Imaginative Ethnography, "Welcome to CIE"
(www.imaginativeethnography.org)

The three methods conventionally considered to form the core of ethnographic research practice are participant observation, interviewing, and analysis of documentary, archival, and scholarly literature. Participant observation, as conventionally practiced, imagines "the ethnographer" as a person who

IMAGE 1.3: Moose art, Niagara-on-the-Lake, Canada.

Credit: Denielle Elliott, 2015.

travels from their own community to another, conducts fieldwork focused on "observations of X group," and then returns home to analyze and communicate the findings—most often to other scholars. Privileged emphasis is granted to "observation" as a source of valid knowledge, with "participation" signaling that the ethnographer's authority rests on having "been there" (Clifford 1983). Rich, careful, and thorough descriptions of what people do and say; when and how they do and say it, and with and to whom; and the consequences of all these continue to be fundamental to ethnographic practice, but how ethnography is carried out and which theoretical insights shape our thinking about it change our understandings of both the practice and the knowledge created.

In 1991, Barbara Tedlock proposed changing the term "participant observation" to "observant participation." This shift in terminology indicates a critique of theories that position researchers as active, observing subjects and research participants as passive, observed objects. Tedlock's reformulation also recognizes the growing number of "insiders" conducting ethnography within what they identify as their own communities, networks, and organizations. The kind of ethnography that we are interested in here is particularly attuned to how bodily and affective experiences are part of ethnographic practice. Performance ethnographer D. Soyini Madison (2006, 401), for example, writes, "Something happens differently when your body must move and adjust to the rhythms, structures, rules, dangers, joys and secrets of a unique location. Ethnography is as much, or more, about bodily attention—performing in and against a circumscribed space—as it is about what is told to you in an interview." New forms of ethnographic writing, she maintains, take seriously the ordinary smells, sounds, and sights, as well as the extraordinary.

We are thus also attentive to the ways in which our own writing practices and ways of knowing are shaped by the affective and the sensorial. For instance, Denielle Elliott ("Writing," this volume) discusses how different forms of writing—poetic, satirical, fictional—can force us to know the world in different ways through unique engagements with the sensory world around us and with our research collaborators. Writing poetically demands a different sort of attention to the world. Dara Culhane's chapter ("Sensing") describes how paying close analytic attention to polysensory experience challenges the conventional Western sensory hierarchy that recognizes only five senses, conceptualizes each as separate and distinct, and considers sight as the privileged source of legitimate knowledge. This is evidenced, for example, by the English expression "seeing is believing" and legal recognition of "eye-witness accounts." Academic conventions reflect this culturally and historically specific approach to knowledge where sights, words, and text are privileged, whereas dynamic interactions among sounds, tastes, odors, touches, senses of place and of belonging and exclusion, and the extrasensory are often ignored or dismissed as irrelevant to social life and the study of knowledge. To take sensory experience, like imagination, as significant in knowledge co-creation constitutes a practice of epistemological and political critique.

Like bodies, feelings were not historically considered to be sources of reliable, valuable knowledge. The contributors to this volume approach affective scholarship as a way to tease out the imagination in social lives, following Sara Ahmed's (2014) proposal that theoretical concepts are most generative when they are embodied, lived, and "sweaty." For instance, Cristina Moretti's chapter ("Walking") considers the ways in which walking can be an ethnographic methodology, one that confronts us with traces, memories, and puzzles that jar our habitual ways of thinking and researching, and that demand different ways of both walking and writing. She shows how guided city walks can draw upon public space as both an object and an embodied site of engagement and inquiry. Alexandrine Boudreault-Fournier's chapter ("Recording and Editing") demonstrates how the development of our "sonic imagination" forces us to listen to and to contend with silences, noises, and voices in our ethnographic fieldwork and to develop new technologies for recording and conveying. For example, she collaborated with Brazilian visual anthropologists to record and produce a sonic and visual account of the 2014 World Cup football match.

Contemporary approaches to interviewing disrupt conventions along these same lines. Moving away from an interrogative model, where a researcher predetermines the focus of an interview and prepares questions, and a research participant's role is to provide raw data in response, the authors here approach interviews as specialized conversations between co-creators in which context, investment in the research project, and relationships between researchers and research participants significantly shape the content. Similarly, documents, archives, and academic literature are explored with critical analytic attention to the political context of their creation and distribution, to their producers' locations and intentions, to researchers' experiences and analyses, and to the multiple possible readings and interpretations diverse audiences may contribute (Burton 2006; Costa 2010). Research "methods" are, therefore, deeply theoretical: the explanatory beliefs (theories) we hold about how knowledge is created, and authorized or dismissed, all shape how we go about conducting our inquiries into meaning making and knowledge co-creation.

How imagination and imaginative practices infuse social relationships constitutes a particular focus of our work. We consider creativity as actively intermingled with imaginative practices, everyday life, and social relationships. We see the potential of creative methodologies to deepen our understandings, enrich our analyses, and facilitate our communication with diverse audiences both in the academy and out.

IMAGE 1.4: "Guardians," Alert Bay, Canada.

Credit: Clifford Emery, 2015.

Imaginative Practices

Argued over for centuries by poets and philosophers, imagination has been in equal measure exalted for its world-shaping power and disparaged for its potentially duplicitous trafficking between reality and illusion.
—*Stuart McLean (2007, 5)*

"Imagination" is a word we all use, often. It stands for activities we all do, frequently. Yet, as you know from your own lived experiences, "imagination" resists fixed definition. Imagination itself, as a concept, evokes a wide range of ideas and responses. For one, it might conjure a memory of an encouraging voice: "Use your imagination!" For another, it might evoke a warning: "Don't let your imagination get the best of you!" And yet another might associate it with fear: "You cannot imagine the horror!" Filmic images of mutilated bodies, aliens, monsters, and zombies flash across screens in cinemas around the world, sparking our imaginations. So, too, do paintings of pastoral scenes hung in silent, austere art galleries, transporting their viewers to other times and places, as might stone tools encased in glass display cabinets in musty museums. If asked to represent and communicate individual experiences of what we call "imagination," some of us might recite lines of poetry, hum beats of music, or execute a dance move. Some might snarl about glossy billboards that pollute public spaces and prey on our imaginations, promising us happiness if only we buy this or that shiny new thing. Others might refer to stories—whether told in books, TV shows, or chance encounters with a stranger—that ask us to imagine what it might feel like to be incarcerated, violated, and hungry; to be free and well fed; to be in love; to die alone. Perhaps, like Sana, our imaginations dance with unconventional fonts, wild margins, images of oil spills, radical research, and hip hop music.

We take the multiple meanings and perpetually generative nature of the concept of "imagination" as its unruly potential—not as errors to be corrected by theory or as obstacles to be overcome by practice. Our use of this term follows anthropologist Stuart McLean's (2007, 6) description of imagination as "an active component of experience and perception, engaged in a constant interchange with the material textures of the existing world." The authors in this volume show how attention to the potentialities of the imagination can force an alternative rendering of social lives, one that accounts for the forgotten, disappeared, hidden, and lost. Cristina Moretti's chapter in this volume, "Walking," shows us how she and her collaborators, who include long-time Italian-born residents and newly arrived immigrants, "co-imagine" diverse pasts, presents, and futures by creating walking tours, together, in Milan, Italy. Dara Culhane challenges us to imagine ourselves as multisensory, embodied, imaginative beings living and dying with others in historically specific and politically charged environments. Alexandrine Boudreault-Fournier considers how new sound and visual technologies imaginatively reconfigure the worlds around us. In her chapter entitled "Writing," Denielle Elliott asks readers to "undiscipline" their imagination as a way to retheorize the quotidian.

"Imagination" has long been a subject of debate in the Western European philosophical tradition, at least since the fourth century BCE, when Aristotle defined imagination as mental imagery of two kinds. The first, "sensitive imagination," is stimulated by sensory experiences like seeing, hearing, smelling, tasting, and touching, experienced through the body. The second, "deliberative imagination," refers to how cognitive capacities—housed in the mind and theorized as absent in the body—analyze, or make sense of, social experience.

Elaborating on Aristotle, René Descartes posited a radical separation between mind and body—known as "Cartesian dualism"—arguing that reason is located in human minds, distinct from human bodies where passion and irrationality lurk. An ever-present threat to the mind's independence from, and putative supremacy over, the body, imagination is an outlaw in the binary regime of Cartesian dualism. Not securely contained within either, but found traveling unpredictably, promiscuously within and between people, always in movement, always in process, imagination persistently hints at the possibility of surprise. Resisting Descartes and the traditional canons of Western philosophy, *A Different Kind of Ethnography* problematizes a radical, abstract separation between mind and body. Here we follow anthropologist Kirsten Hastrup (1994, 232) when she writes that if we consider our lived experience as a legitimate source of knowledge, it becomes immediately evident that the limitations of language confound us: "We lack the words for, rather than the experience of, the unity of body and mind," she writes.

Imagination's presumed vulnerability to bodily desires and affective intensities, and its refusal to be theoretically contained, renders it symbolically and materially dangerous to ruling political regimes and challenging to conventional Western philosophy and social theory. Only later did the imagination come to be associated with creativity, valued for its potential to liberate thinking, to "make the absent present" (Mittermaier 2011, 17), and as a means to illuminate. In these later renderings, imagination is seen as a process and relational, not as an object. Anthropologists interested in imagination conventionally focused their research on domains designated within the Western academy as imaginative/not rational: the arts, religion, cosmology, ritual, shamanic healing, dreams, and ceremony.

Sneath, Holbraad, and Pedersen (2009, 5) begin their introduction to a special issue of the journal *Ethnos* devoted to "Imagination and Anthropology" with the question, "What would an anthropology that takes imagination seriously look like?"

They critique much contemporary work for considering imagination as overly instrumental, focused on how it serves functional roles in peoples' lives, and/or as overly romantic, considered only in terms of its positive features. They argue instead for an approach that focuses on "the social and material means by which particular imaginings are generated" (6). The work you will read here focuses on the potential of imagination, but we do so mindful of anthropologist Jamie Saris's caution (2007, 59): "If we really believe that imagination is to be one of the midwives of 'another world,' then we are over-late in investigating how it is under-girding and reproducing the one in which we currently find ourselves."

Philosophical debates about how "imagination" may be understood are important and currently attract a good deal of scholarly attention and energy. As ethnographers, we pay close, critical attention to what people we work with call "imagination" and to the projects they take up in its name. In other words, we look for the meanings of imagination less in abstract philosophy and more in how these meanings emerge in action. The "doing" of imagination is what we call "imaginative practices."

The current shift of attention to methodology is also evident in studies of imagination. Anthropologist Vincent Crapanzano (2004, 1), for example, writes, "anthropologists have been less concerned with imaginative processes than with the products of the imagination." In this book, we turn our attention precisely to these processes, inspired by current work on imagination in anthropology. Andrea Muehlebach, for example, explores relationships between precarity and the ethical imagination as she asks "what the task of ethnography is now that 'things are falling apart, again'" (2013, 297). Tine Gammeltoft (2014, 117) investigates "how people's fantasies, fears and imaginings blend with the workings of state power" in her ethnography of disability experience in Vietnam; and Didier Fassin (2014) analyzes the play of imagination as life story-telling transgresses conventional boundaries between ethnography and fiction.

In this book, and in our work as a whole, we treat imagination as a social practice, integral to relationships among people(s) and between people(s) and the cultural, political, and ecological environments with which we are entangled. We approach the imaginative as "anticipatory" (Crapanzano 2004, 20) or like "ellipses" (Berlant 2014), both characterized by uncertainty, an expectation not yet fulfilled, a not knowing that is liberating in its potential and possibility. The imaginative realm is not limited to representation as images, text, dreams, or memory that confines its interpretation to object or subject. But when approached as a process or practice, as something relational and productive, imagination leads to new spaces of inquiry, spaces that are dependent on the collaborative nature of anthropological knowledge. Such an approach situates imagination as a pedagogy, and one with the potential to open up and to make visible the unknown.

Creative Methodologies

*Treating creativity as a social and cultural process . . . [brings] . . . into
critical focus the limitations entailed in conceptualizing creativity as a
form of invention exercised by the autonomous individual . . .*
—Tim Ingold and Elizabeth Hallam (2007, 20)

Like "imagination," "creativity" invokes ideas, practices, desires, and forces; it
defies a single, fixed definition. Like "imagination," "creativity" is a common
word that we see, hear, and speak frequently, and it is hard to define with
words alone; it is always more, but never less, than what language can represent. Like "imagination," here "creativity" is a process, valued in its mundane
as well as spectacular manifestations, practiced in diverse ways by experts and
amateurs, sometimes in extraordinary activity and sometimes in the ordinary
demands of human survival.

"Creativity" can include, but is not limited to, what we generally consider
making art: painting, drawing, filming, weaving, sculpting, carving, singing,
dancing, making music, and performing. Yet, creativity can emerge in ordinary places and mundane practices too. Don't cooks bring creativity to feeding
people every day, as well as to preparing gourmet feasts? Don't we all bring
creativity to how we dress and adorn ourselves, to how we furnish our homes,
to how we balance (or not) our budgets, to how we express our feelings about
other people, events, the future? How then might we bring creativity into our
ethnographic research?

In this book, as with imagination, rather than debate what creativity is,
we focus on the work that creativity does, both in the world in general and
in ethnographic research in particular. Working with creative methodologies, inquiring into imaginative practices—this constitutes *A Different Kind of
Ethnography*. This combination of imagination, creativity, and ethnography has
the potential, we believe, to deepen, complicate, and extend our inquiry into
how people make, repair, and remake the world.

We are inspired by many creative projects that bridge the visual arts, theater,
performance, film, sound studies, and critical scholarship. T.L. Cowan's experimental, activist, feminist performances draw on satire, burlesque, stand-up
comedy, and queer theory to challenge gender, sexuality, and aging norms.[1]
Her genre-bending, multimedia installations are grounded in scholarly critiques
and experimental art practices that seriously take up challenges of creativity
and the imaginative. So too does the work of Max Liboiron, activist, artist, and
sociologist, who uses (and transforms) historical drawings, experimental
photography, dioramas, collagraphy, multimedia installations, and more in her
explorations of ecology, climate change, science, nature, and discard studies.[2]

In film and sound, we see similar boundary-breaking work with Lucien Castaing-Taylor and Véréna Paravel's *Leviathan* (2012), an experimental ethnographic film of sound and sight in US fishing practices off New England. Dance ethnographers like Karen Barbour (2011), Theresa Buckland (2013), Dena Davida (2011), Judith Hamera (2007), and many others bring a wealth of experience to studies of movement and embodied knowledge entangled in histories and contemporary communities. Performance ethnographer Soyini Madison (2010) advances the political potential of performance in international human rights activism. Contributors to a recent collection edited by Alex Flynn and Jonas Tinius (2015) offer critical analyses of how the transformative potential of performance is facilitated and thwarted in international and community development programs. All of these are transdisciplinary, exploratory efforts in which artistic and anthropological modes of inquiry inform and transform each other, contributing to a different kind of ethnographic practice.

Some of the authors here present their own efforts to combine art and anthropology. Alexandrine Boudreault-Fournier discusses the creativity involved in montage editing of sound and image in her chapter "Recording and Editing." For her, the process of recording and the editing techniques of montage together generate worlds in which spectators and listeners can re-imagine the places, events, atmospheres, and activities (among other things) that are represented in a film or a sound clip. In "Performing," Magdalena Kazubowski-Houston dives into the fairy tale genre through a collaborative research project with Polish Roma. Denielle Elliott highlights how a little creativity in thinking might transform a pile of dirty dishes in the kitchen sink into ethnographic stories of fracking, depression, immigration, and more. Cristina Moretti discusses how a walk around Milan can give rise to creative storytelling, mixing narrative autoethnographic accounts with speculation about the lives of others in shared spaces. Dara Culhane's chapter on sensing explores how creative methodologies are engaged in evoking and representing sensory experience in ethnographic practice. In sum, while the kind of ethnography we propose builds on conventional methods like participant observation, interviewing, and documentary research, we do so with questions informed by new approaches to collaboration and with attention to relationships between theory and method that are conceptualized as problems in epistemology, all organized around the question, How do we know what we know?

Contributions to this collection emerge from contemporary work that takes as its starting point the premise that methodology and theory are necessarily dynamic, mutually constitutive—you cannot have one without the other—and irreducibly entangled. In critically analyzing the theory/method, methodology, and epistemology debates, we join with others across the arts, humanities, and social sciences who are challenging convention and developing relational theories of epistemology that focus on intersubjectivity and subscribe to the idea that human beings are most productively understood as social beings who come to know what we know, about both ourselves and others, in and through relationship. We make each other up.

We write this volume in the tradition of anthropologists before us who have aimed to "destroy prejudices, open horizons, and promote creative thought and action" (Crapanzano 2004, 3), and to encourage social and cultural critique that is attentive to the everyday and the extraordinary, the sensorial, the forgotten, the obvious, the messy. We build on these critiques by considering sensory, embodied and affective knowledge to be significant, by questioning conventional theoretical frameworks, and by working with critical approaches in reassembling, reimagining, and rebuilding the discipline, by proposing *A Different Kind of Ethnography*.

References

Ahmed, Sara. 2014. *Willful Subjects*. Durham, NC: Duke University Press. http://dx.doi.org/10.1215/9780822376101

Barbour, Karen. 2011. *Dancing across the Page: Narrative and Embodied Ways of Knowing*. London: Intellect.

Behar, Ruth, and Deborah Gordon. 1991. *Women Writing Culture*. Berkeley: University of California Press.

Berlant, Lauren. 2014. "Living in Ellipsis: On Biopolitics and the Attachment to Life." Paper presented at the Ioan Davies Memorial Lecture, York University, Toronto, 15 October.

Biehl, João. 2013. "Ethnography in the Way of Theory." *Cultural Anthropology* 28 (4): 573–97. http://dx.doi.org/10.1111/cuan.12028

Biolsi, Thomas. 1997. *Indians and Anthropologists: Vine Deloria Jr. and the Critique of Anthropology*. Tucson: University of Arizona Press.

Bodley, John H. 2008. *Anthropology and Contemporary Human Problems*. Lanham, MD: Alta Mira.

Boyer, Dominic, and George Marcus. 2015. "Introduction." In *Theory Can Be More Than It Used to Be: Learning Anthropology's Method in a Time of Transition*, eds. Dominic Boyer, James Faubion, and George Marcus, 1–12. Ithaca, NY: Cornell University Press.

Brodine, Maria, Craig Campbell, Kate Hennessy, Fiona P. McDonald, Trudi Lynn Smith, and Stephanie Takaragawa. 2011. "Ethnographic Terminalia: An Introduction." *Visual Anthropology Review* 27 (1): 49–51. http://dx.doi.org/10.1111/j.1548-7458.2011.01078.x

Buckland, Theresa. 2013. "Dance and Cultural Memory: Interpreting Fin de Siècle Performances of 'Olde England.'" *Dance Research* 31 (1): 29–66. http://dx.doi.org/10.3366/drs.2013.0058

Burton, Antoinette. 2006. *Archive Stories: Facts, Fictions and the Writing of History*. Durham, NC: Duke University Press. http://dx.doi.org/10.1215/9780822387046

Castaing-Taylor, Lucien, and Véréna Paravel, dirs. 2012. *Leviathan*. 87 min. Cambridge, MA: Harvard Sensory Ethnography Lab.

Castañeda, Quetzil. 2006. "The Invisible Theatre of Ethnography: Performative Principles of Fieldwork. Social Thought and Commentary." *Anthropological Quarterly* 79 (1): 75–104. http://dx.doi.org/10.1353/anq.2006.0004

Cerwonka, Allaine. 2007. "Nervous Conditions: The Stakes in Interdisciplinary Research." In *Improvising Theory: Process and Temporality in Ethnographic Fieldwork*, ed. Allaine Cerwonka and Liisa Malkki, 1–41. Chicago: University of Chicago Press. http://dx.doi.org/10.7208/chicago/9780226100289.001.0001

Clifford, James. 1983. "On Ethnographic Authority." *Representations* 2 (Spring): 118–46. http://dx.doi.org/10.2307/2928386

Clifford, James, and George Marcus. 1986. *Writing Culture: The Poetics and Politics of Ethnography*. Berkeley: University of California Press.

Costa, Maria Cristina Castilho. 2010. "Ethnography of Archives: Between Past and Present." *MATRIZes* 3 (2): 171–86. http://dx.doi.org/10.11606/issn.1982-8160.v3i2p171-186

Crapanzano, Vincent. 2004. *Imaginative Horizons: An Essay in Literary-Philosophical Anthropology*. Chicago: University of Chicago Press.

Davida, Dena. 2011. *Fields in Motion: Ethnography in the Worlds of Dance*. Waterloo, ON: Wilfrid Laurier University Press.

Davis, Dána-Ain, and Christa Craven. 2016. *Feminist Ethnography: Thinking through Methodologies, Challenges, and Possibilities*. London: Rowman & Littlefield.

Ethnographic Terminalia. n. d. "Prospectus." http://ethnographicterminalia.org/about

Fassin, Didier. 2013. "Why Ethnography Matters: On Anthropology and Its Publics." *Cultural Anthropology* 28 (4): 621–46. http://dx.doi.org/10.1111/cuan.12030

Fassin, Didier. 2014. "True Life, Real Lives and Revisiting the Boundaries between Ethnography and Fiction." *American Ethnologist* 41 (1): 40–55. http://dx.doi.org/10.1111/amet.12059

Faubion, James D., and George E. Marcus. 2009. *Fieldwork Is Not What It Used to Be: Learning Anthropology's Method in a Time of Transition*. Ithaca, NY: Cornell University Press.

Flynn, Alex, and Jonas Tinius, eds. 2015. *Anthropology, Theatre, and Development: The Transformative Potential of Performance*. Basingstoke, UK: Palgrave Macmillan. http://dx.doi.org/10.1057/9781137350602

Gammeltoft, Tine. 2014. "Toward an Anthropology of the Imaginary: Specters of Disability in Vietnam." *Ethos* 42 (2): 153–74. http://dx.doi.org/10.1111/etho.12046

Geertz, Clifford. 1998. "Deep Hanging Out." *New York Review of Books* 45(16): 69–72, 22 October.

Ghosh, Amitav. 1994. *In an Antique Land: History in the Guise of a Traveler's Tale*. London: Granta.

Green, Bill, and Nick Hopwood. 2015. "Introduction: Body/Practice?" In *The Body in Professional Practice: Learning and Education, Professional and Practice-based Learning, Series 11*, ed. Bill Green and Nick Hopwood, 3–27. Cham, Switzerland: Springer International.

Hamera, Judith. 2007. *Dancing Communities: Performance, Difference, and Connection in the Global City*. London: Palgrave.

Hastrup, Kirsten. 1994. "Anthropological Knowledge Incorporated: A Discussion." In *Social Experience and Anthropological Knowledge*, eds. Kirsten Hastrup and Peter Hervick, 224–37. London: Routledge. http://dx.doi.org/10.4324/9780203449646_chapter_12

Ingold, Tim. 2008. "Bindings against Boundaries: Entanglements of Life in an Open World." *Environment & Planning A* 40 (8): 1796–810. http://dx.doi.org/10.1068/a40156

Ingold, Tim, and Elizabeth Hallam. 2007. "Creativity and Cultural Improvisation: An Introduction." In *Creativity and Cultural Improvisation*, ed. Elizabeth Hallam and Tim Ingold, 1–24. Oxford: Berg.

Katzman, Erika R. 2015. "Embodied Reflexivity: Knowledge and the Body in Professional Practice." In *The Body in Professional Practice: Learning and Education, Professional and Practice-Based Learning, Series 11*, eds. Bill Green and Nick Hopwood, 157–72. Cham, Switzerland: Springer International. http://dx.doi.org/10.1007/978-3-319-00140-1_10

Kottak, Conrad P. 1999. "The New Ecological Anthropology." *American Anthropologist* 101 (1): 23–35. http://dx.doi.org/10.1525/aa.1999.101.1.23

Lewin, Ellen, and W.L. Leap. 2001. *Out in Public: Reinventing Lesbian/Gay Anthropology in a Globalizing World*. Chichester, UK: John Wiley & Sons.

Madison, D. Soyini. 2006. "Staging Fieldwork/Performing Human Rights." In *The Sage Handbook of Performance Studies*, eds. D. Soyini Madison and Judith Hamera, 397–419. London: Sage. http://dx.doi.org/10.4135/9781412976145.n23

Madison, D. Soyini. 2010. *Acts of Activism: Human Rights as Radical Performance*. Cambridge: Cambridge University Press. http://dx.doi.org/10.1017/CBO9780511675973

Mahmood, Saba. 2011. *Politics of Piety: The Islamic Revival and the Feminist Subject*. Princeton, NJ: Princeton University Press.

Marcus, George. 2012. "The Legacies of Writing Culture and the Near Future of the Ethnographic Form: A Sketch." *Cultural Anthropology* 27(3): 427–45.

McLean, Stuart. 2007. "Introduction: Why Imagination?" *Irish Journal of Anthropology* 10 (2): 5–9.

Mittermaier, Amira. 2011. *Dreams That Matter: Egyptian Landscapes of the Imagination*. Berkeley: University of California Press.

Morris, Courtney Desiree. 2015. "Where It Hurts: 2014 Year In Review." *American Anthropologist* 117 (3): 540–52. http://dx.doi.org/10.1111/aman.12284

Muehlebach, Andrea. 2013. "On Precariousness and the Ethical Imagination: The Year 2012 in Sociocultural Anthropology." *American Anthropologist* 115 (2): 297–311. http://dx.doi.org/10.1111/aman.12011

Said, Edward. 1989. "Representing the Colonized: Anthropology's Interlocutors."
Critical Inquiry 15 (2): 205–25. http://dx.doi.org/10.1086/448481

Said, Edward. 1993. *Culture and Imperialism*. New York: Knopf.

Saris, A. Jamie. 2007. "Culture, Inequality and the Bureaucratic Imagination: States and
Subjects for a New Millennium." *Irish Journal of Anthropology* 10 (2): 54–60.

Schneider, Arnd, and Christopher Wright. 2006. *Contemporary Art and Anthropology*.
Oxford: Berg Publishers.

Schneider, Arnd, and Christopher Wright, eds. 2013. *Anthropology and Art Practice*.
London: Bloomsbury.

Simpson, Audra. 2014. *Mohawk Interruptus: Political Life across the Border of Settler States*.
Durham, NC: Duke University Press. http://dx.doi.org/10.1215/9780822376781

Smith, Linda. 1999. *Decolonizing Methodologies: Research and Indigenous Peoples*. London:
Zed Books.

Sneath, David, Martin Holbraad, and Morten Axel Pedersen. 2009. "Technologies of the
Imagination: An Introduction." *Ethnos* 74 (1): 5–30. http://dx.doi.org/10.1080/
00141840902751147

Stoller, Paul. 1992. *The Cinematic Griot: The Ethnography of Jean Rouch*. Chicago: University
of Chicago Press.

Tedlock, Barbara. 1991. "From Participant Observation to the Observation of
Participation: The Emergence of Narrative Ethnography." *Journal of Anthropological
Research* 47 (1): 69–94. http://dx.doi.org/10.1086/jar.47.1.3630581

Turner, Victor, and Richard Schechner. 1988. *The Anthropology of Performance*. New York:
PAJ Publications.

Westmoreland, Mark. 2013. "Making Sense: Affective Research in Postwar Lebanese
Art." *Critical Arts* 27 (6): 717–36. http://dx.doi.org/10.1080/02560046.2013.867593

Notes

1 See her work at http://tlcowan.net.

2 See her work at http://maxliboiron.com.

CHAPTER 2

WRITING

Denielle Elliott

IMAGE 2.1: Mural and graffiti, Paris, France.

Credit: Denielle Elliott, 2013.

Writing never ceases to amaze me.
    —Michael Jackson (2013, 93)

Undisciplining the Imagination

What does it mean to write imaginatively, or to write with imagination? Kenyan
writer Binyavanga Wainaina (2011), reflecting on his childhood, writes about the

role of colonialism in disciplining African children and their imaginations with the expectation that they be "good boys." This admonition rubs up against his own imagination, which seems rather unruly and wild, which wants to explore, disrupt, and free itself. In his video essay "We Must Free Our Imaginations," he says, "I want to live a life with a free imagination . . . to make new exciting things."[1] How can we do this in anthropology? What might an imaginative ethnography look like? As Dominic Boyer (2016) explains, twenty-first century anthropology demands that anthropologists be rather prolific writers, as we are expected to write academic journal articles, publish books, and contribute to public anthropology debates in online and news forums. Yet, as Joshua Rothman recently summarized, academic writing is often "knotty and strange, remote and insular, technical and specialized, forbidding and clannish" (Rothman 2014). Undergraduate students often find required readings from academic journals difficult to comprehend and hard to relate to in their abstraction. But it doesn't have to be this way. There are many examples within cultural anthropology of writing that reaches audiences outside of the academy, that blurs and bends genres, and that is accessible, creative, and imaginative. But Rothman's critique and other recent debates about academic writing do raise important questions for the ethnographer as writer. How do we write ethnography?[2] What sorts of disciplinary traditions shape our practice? What sorts of things do we pay attention to in our writing? What sorts of things do we deliberately leave out? In this chapter, I think about the anthropologist as writer (Geertz 1989; Wulff 2016), in order to trace various paths that anthropologists have taken in their attempts to write with both effect and affect.

This chapter is concerned with both form and content—how we write and what we write about. I want to distinguish between (1) writing in an imaginative way (experimenting with form), and (2) writing about ideas that engage seriously with imagination. Form is perhaps the easier of the two to address: we can write ethnographic poetry, creative nonfiction, fictional ethnography, and memoirs. We can blur fiction and criticism, draw field notes, or partition essays into a series of tweets. Imaginatively engaging with content is more difficult, but there are multiple ways in which we might experiment— in form and content, in structure and style—while remaining committed to an ethnographic narrative, one that emerges from in-depth, collaborative, rigorous fieldwork, which aims to engage and transform. In this essay, I am interested in exploring a specific form of anthropological writing, an imaginative ethnography that is informed by literary creative practice, one that tells different types of stories and pays attention to different sorts of experiences.

Influenced by creative writing and fiction, embracing the 1990s focus on narrative, and recognizing important critiques of anthropology (Clifford 1986; Clifford and Marcus 1986), sociocultural anthropologists began experimenting with narrative-based ethnographies that privileged marginalized and subaltern women's critiques of local, national, and global politics. Works such as Ruth Behar's *Translated Woman* (1993) and *Vulnerable Observer* (1996), Lila Abu-Lughod's *Writing Women's Worlds* (1993), Marjorie Shostak's *Nisa* (1981), and Karen Brown's *Mama Lola* (2001) are important examples of how powerful narratives could theorize the world while also attempting to reconcile the challenges of "speaking for others" (Alcoff 1991; Behar and Gordon 1995). Such examples remind us that writing is personal, political, and pedagogical (Rajabali 2014). They also remind us that storytelling is a powerful means to theorize the world in which we live and that there are many ways to tell a story.

Some forms of writing are blurred and interdisciplinary by nature, such as auto-ethnography, poetic ethnography, and fictional ethnography. There is a comprehensive body of literature that discusses both ethnographic fiction and fictional accounts of anthropological fieldwork.[3] This chapter focuses instead on a form of ethnographic writing that borrows from many creative writing strategies to produce what we call "imaginative ethnography." Others have characterized "ethnographic fiction" as a form of writing in which the writer borrows strategies from fiction and creative nonfiction, like storytelling and imagining, to convey cultural experience and everyday lives (see, for instance, Hecht 2007). Such writing, I argue, should not be deemed fictional at all—rather, storytelling, imagining, and ethnographic writing should be understood as integral and essential to a contemporary anthropology that matters.

In spite of the inspirational and daring work of the 1990s, and the call for a different kind of ethnography by James Clifford and George Marcus (1986), many anthropologists have abandoned experimental and imaginative writing practices. Positivist and conservative strategies, preferred by the academy and by scholarly journals that shy away from unorthodox, unconventional, or genre-bending papers, have found favor. Such accounts are often alienating to the general reader, appealing only to a small, elite cadre of academics—and they fail to capture the messy, sensorial experience of everyday life.

The Imaginative Path

As an anthropologist, I find my inspiration for writing imaginatively in those who write fiction and creative nonfiction. Novelists like Nadine Gordimer (1989), Binyavanga Wainaina (2011), and Lee Maracle (1996) write stories about social inequities and historical violence, and do so with emotional honesty, artistry, and skill. Other novelists poignantly touch on the wide range of anthropological concerns: migration, racial politics, sexuality, gender norms, urbanization, dispossession, histories of colonialism, class tensions, diaspora, kinship, and more, and yet fiction is often deemed nontheoretical. I suggest that creative forms of writing might "do theory" considerably better than traditional forms of sociocultural anthropology, as it is often written in a language that is accessible to a much wider audience. Like ethnography, fiction forces us to think differently about the world by challenging what we thought we knew.

Dian Million (2011, 315) argues that "theory, narrative, and critical thinking are not exclusive of each other." Stories in either form have the potential to disrupt how we think about processes, practices, and people. As a number of Indigenous scholars have argued, stories are a form of theory, even as they take shape as affective narratives (see, for instance, Christian 1987; Million 2011, 2014). Audra Simpson and Andrea Smith (2014, 7) explain, "if we demystify theory to understand it as the thinking behind why we think and do things, it is clear that all peoples, of course, 'do' theory." Creative writing and ethnography have transformative potential to shift relations of power, as so many anticolonial and feminist writings clearly demonstrate. Both can give voice to those who are denied forums for speaking or are silenced altogether. Both can be factual, based on historical realities, and yet evoke imaginaries that we might only dream of.

Creative writing is often both subtler and more precise than ethnography, honest in a way that conventionally written ethnographic texts rarely are. The very thing that makes for good ethnography—complex relationships developed over long periods of time—also makes writing difficult. Writing about the lives of those with whom we work, become friends, and sometimes live is challenging, as any anthropologist will attest. In its claim to be made up, and not representative of "real" lives, fiction gives authors space to write truthfully about provocative issues and experiences without destroying relationships (Elliott forthcoming, 2014). Fiction writers can go places that ethnographers choose not to, and thus can be more comprehensive and searching. And fiction doesn't couch truths in inaccessible academic jargon. For these reasons, creative writing can open up a route toward imaginative ethnography.

We are experiencing shifts in reading and writing—blogs, webpages, emails, SMS, Twitter, Facebook, Instagram—and these new technologies and forms of communication are seeping into the ways students learn and study, and the ways faculty teach and engage with students. They are also changing the possibilities for how we as anthropologists share and convey our research to others, including the communities where we work. More accessible in some cases, they may liberate ethnographic writing from the conservative rules and restrictions that continue to govern our writing practices.

I have always struggled with writing academically. I felt intimidated by the academic texts and scholarly articles that we read in graduate school; I lacked confidence in my own writing and analytical skills, and I could not find my voice in the sorts of academic products demanded of me. I found it particularly difficult to write about other people's work, which is essentially what we do in undergraduate and graduate studies, until we finally get to do our own research. We write literature reviews, we write analytical reviews, we write précis. By the third year of my PhD program, I was quite confident about one thing: I would never finish my studies because I was unable to write. Writing is challenging for many people, faculty and students alike. And for good reason: there are big expectations of us. We are trusted with the deeply personal stories of others. We rely on the memory of others to tell us their stories and then on our own to retell their stories. We must translate, and not just from one language to another. We strive to make sense of what others tell us and then to figure out how to write their stories in a way that is sensitive, critical, and compelling, all at once. This chapter examines a handful of contemporary ethnographies that do just this and imagines other possibilities that may not yet exist.

Writing Imaginatively in Form

Writing as doing displaces writing as meaning; writing becomes meaningful in the material, dis/continuous act of writing.
—Della Pollock (1998, 75)

Contemporary ethnographers are borrowing from poetry, creative nonfiction, narrative prose, poetry, testimonials, and storytelling. And there is a long and rich history of scholars who have experimented with writing forms and styles, helping to transform disciplinary norms and unsettle genre boundaries. Anthropologists have in different ways played with the structure and form of ethnographic writing. For example, Tobias Hecht wrote fiction, in *After Life: An Ethnographic Novel* (2006); Paul Stoller authored a memoir, *Stranger in the Village of the Sick: A Memoir of Cancer, Sorcery, and Healing* (2005); and Anand Pandian and his grandfather M.P. Mariappan collaborated on an ethnographic biography (2014). In this section, I consider novel, emerging imaginative forms including ethnographic poetry, animations, satire, and experimental writing mediated by technology, such as Twitter essays.

Writing Poetically
I don't know anything anymore
except this:
If Knowledge came to me
in the thickest part of the night,
woke me with a flashlight,

asked me, What do you know?
I would say, nothing, nothing at all,
except diving, and loving this world.
                —Adrie Kusserow (2002, 50)

How might we think about ethnographic poetry? How is it different from other forms of poetry? To write an ethnographic poem is to convey our knowledge, our observations, and our theoretical analyses in the poetic form. Kent Maynard (2009, 115) asks, "How does writing poetry help us know more about society, about other forms of discourse and practice?" For Renato Rosaldo (2013, 101), ethnographic poetry, or *antropoesía*, is situated in "social and cultural worlds; [it is] poetry that is centrally about the human condition." This form offers possibilities for knowing and representing the world in a way that is not only more lyrical, but also more affective in the way that emotions can be portrayed and evoked.

There is a small but growing body of published ethnographic poetry and lyrical prose that includes work by Kent Maynard (2001, 2002, 2009), E. Valentine Daniel (1996, 2013), Renato Rosaldo (2013), Adrie Kusserow (2002, 2014), and Melisa Cahnmann-Taylor[4] (2013). (We can assume there also are multitudes of unpublished and incomplete poems in notebooks, laptops, and field notes.) Maynard (2009) suggests that, although not without its own challenges, ethnographic poetry offers something important to anthropology and to knowing the world. He argues that ethnographic poetry may sometimes be better suited than prose to understanding the world because much of life is connected to the rhythmic, poetic, or musical. Prose rarely accounts for the affective dimension—happiness, grief, desire, rage, malaise—nor does it necessarily allow us to convey uncertainties, contradictions, or ironies in the lives we witness.

E. Valentine Daniel's (2013) "The Coolie: An Unfinished Epic" is an example of what imaginative ethnography might look like as an ethnohistorical poem.[5] Writing in iambic hexameter[6] about Tamil plantation workers in Sri Lanka, Daniel evokes memory, emotion, and the senses while maintaining ethnographic rigor and historical accuracy. Of his discovery of the poetic form and the challenges of writing in academic prose, he writes that there was "[a] truth in verse that could not be conveyed in prose, a truth that was present at hand in oral history and ethnography but made distant or secondary in prose. I believe that most prose in the social sciences in particular does not merely overshadow or repress this affective truth in its secondary status but may even kill it" (Daniel 2013, 68).

In contrast to academic prose that can stifle and hide more than it illuminates, ethnographic poetry can evoke that which is often left hidden in ethnography, as Melisa Cahnmann-Taylor (2006) does in her poem about inner-city students and the failure of American schooling.

Ghetto Teachers' Apology

I'm afraid, sweet Wilmarie, we've lied.
We didn't teach you how to hide
your Rite Aid salary from Welfare
in a Dominican bank. We didn't tell
you how to find a roommate or put a lock
on your bedroom door or how to walk
after sundown by yourself, how to slouch
at your brother's funeral, patched
bullet holes in an open casket in your living room.
We never told you,
like your boss, you can't speak English,
or like your cousin, you can't speak Spanish.
We didn't tell you how to live on
$5.50 an hour or that at seventeen
you'd be an orphan. We didn't want to sour
our hopes and fictions, we wanted you to flower,
and prove us wrong. Sweet Wilmarie,
we're sorry.
We didn't live on your side of town
between crack houses and crackdowns.
We're not like you, we didn't know how to survive
behind shatter proof glass with those pretty brown eyes.

Writing poetically is not only about form but also about content. Maynard (2009, 121) explains: "Rather than treat emotion as ornamental of, or incidental to, economic, political or other instrumental acts, perhaps, poetry can show us how affect may even be constituent of economic and political life." This is evidenced most noticeably in the work of Renato Rosaldo (2013, 88), who published a collection of essays about the accident and death of his first wife, Michelle Rosaldo, in 1981, and his grief, mourning, and sense of loss in the aftermath.

Colored Marshmallows

In Bayombong Father Joe arranges
for Shelly's body to be transported to Manila.
We wait in a windowless room.
Sam lies listless on my lap,
asks for stories, one after another.

> I buy colored marshmallows
> for Manny who glistens red
> and screams and screams.

Ethnographic poetry offers possibilities for an anthropology that takes seriously the complexity and enormity of human emotions, and allows a poetic voice that is critical and theoretical (Maynard 2009). Critical scholarly work can combine both academic prose and the poetic voice, for example, Dian Million's "There Is a River in Me" (2014) and the iconic *Borderlands/La Frontera: The New Mestiza* by Gloria Anzaldúa (1987). The poetic voice can be used to challenge the hegemony of academic and colonial language and can privilege affect as central to the human condition.

As ethnographic writing, poetry, like the other forms discussed here, is no less demanding in our attempts to balance "wellcrafted, artful verse" with "validity in its research results" (Maynard and Cahnmann-Taylor 2010, 12). Whether narrative, lyrical, traditional, or free form, an artful ethnographic poem must be honest, and it must tell a story. Stuart McLean (2009) offers a theoretically nuanced account of how anthropologists might make use of the poetic and calls on anthropologists to reconceptualize the ways in which stories are formed. McLean (2009) argues "not for a 'cultural poetics,' but for a more broadly conceived poetics of making" (215), one that is "experimental, multiagentive, and pluralistic" (213). He maps out avenues for thinking about imaginative forms and for "practicing creativity" (216), forms that are attuned to history and philosophy in the ways in which stories are retold. In his recent work, he merges poetic language, visual expression, and acoustic material to explore ontologies of the sea (McLean, forthcoming).

Drawing

Although this chapter focuses primarily on writing in text form (whether it is typed on your grandfather's old typewriter, tapped out on your tablet, or written cursively in longhand with a pen), I want to highlight recent work that includes drawing and animation, and to note the growing popularity of graphic novels and graphic animation in anthropology. In scholarly accounts, Tim Ingold (2011), Lynda Barry (2008), and Michael Taussig (2011) have taken up drawing, graphic novels, and animation as serious mediums for deepening our knowledge and for translating our research to a larger public audience (also see Hendrickson 2008). Although animation has a long history in fiction and other popular forms of writing, it has remained marginal in anthropology and the academy more generally.

In *Redrawing Anthropology*, Tim Ingold (2011) argues for the development of a "graphic anthropology" that brings together the materiality of life and culture, a theory of things, ethnographic analysis, and a creative rendering of the world. Drawing what we see and experience during fieldwork and research requires a different sort of attention to the world, one that is affective and sensorial in its demand to take notice of the subtle and not-so-subtle corporeality of everyday life. While drawing is in some ways similar to photography, film (see Alexandrine Boudreault-Fournier's chapter, "Recording and Editing," in this volume), and poetry, the act of drawing, like the act of writing with a pen on paper, is performative and embodied in a specific way. Jessica Taylor (2012, 2) explains that in her research and engagement with drawing "it involved an intense consciousness of self and other; a consciousness of the self within the gaze of the other." Similarly, Taussig argues, "drawing intervenes in the reckoning of reality in ways that writing and photography do not" (2011, 13). Drawing demands a different kind of seeing, one that we need to be trained in and become accustomed to. Sousanis (2015) even suggests that in some cases words limit what we can see and what we understand about the world. Images may also evoke different responses from the audience, given their ability to represent things that simply exceed language—the horrors of genocides, senseless deaths of migrants drowning in the Mediterranean, or extremist attacks on students.

There are few models of ethnographic drawing within the academy.[7] Nick Sousanis (2015) published his dissertation as a graphic novel, *Unflattening*, with Harvard University Press. He argues that drawing doesn't simply make academic scholarship accessible to a larger public audience; something much more profound happens. When drawings and prose are "woven together, in the unique way that comics make possible, one is able to fill in the gaps that the other doesn't address, and they speak to one another—text informs image, image adds meaning to text—a kind of resonance that keeps cycling back and forth."[8] Aleksandra Bartoszko and colleagues (2010) published a study of public spaces and information technology at Oslo University College as a comic book. They explain that the drawings and cartoon character of their work allows for the use of irony, satire, and humor to make sense of the experiences described by the research participants. As it moves from something we witness to something we inscribe, something is both gained and lost in the practice of drawing life, just as with writing life, whether in poetry or prose. Through pencil or charcoal on paper, an image appears, with texture, layers, lines. This emergent area of experimental scholarship offers limitless possibilities for an imaginative ethnography (for instance, see Causey 2016).

And Other Experiments

Recent communication technologies and platforms, like smartphones and Twitter, have transformed how we think about effective communication by introducing a new art of "micro-writing" (Johnson 2011). Although such experiments are becoming increasingly commonplace in many venues, university settings often remain resistant to such transformations. We get used to telling stories in one particular way, as Sana, our introductory interlocutor complained: a written expository essay, in Times New Roman 12-point font. But there are other ways to tell ethnographic stories, other ways to communicate our knowledge. Take Twitter or text messaging (or SMS, short messaging system) as a new medium for communicating (Stommel 2012). Twitter allows a maximum of 140 characters in a "tweet," SMS 160 in a text. Although critics initially suggested that these forms would result in a "devaluing" of language, some studies have suggested that tweets often convey complex ideas with more polysyllabic words than the average sentence structure (Cougnon and Fairon 2014). And even when they don't, we see a new form of language emerging, what Jill Walker Rettberg calls "SMS speak."[9]

Rettberg draws attention to a post she read on CNN's website, in which a teacher was complaining about a student's writing. The student had been asked to detail what she did over her summer break. The student's essay began: "My smmr hols wr CWOT. B4, we used 2go2 NY 2C my bro, his GF & thr 3:- kids FTF. ILNY, it's a gr8 plc." For the traditionalists and language conservative this may seem like a bastardization of the language. In translation it reads: "My summer holidays were a complete waste of time. Before, we used to go to New York to see my brother, his girlfriend and their three screaming kids face to face. I love New York. It's a great place." The student's version, as Rettberg points out, is playful and creative. She combines regular words, numerical characters, abbreviations, and letters to convey the same idea as the full sentence but does so in a way that imagines the possibilities of language outside of the expository essay. Although such a style will not be embraced or welcomed by all classrooms, professors, or publishing venues, we can work to create spaces that allow and encourage students and ourselves to experiment with mischievous writing.

Novelist Teju Cole has also turned to experimenting with Twitter essays.[10] In "A Piece of the Wall" he constructs a 4,000-word, nonfiction essay focusing on immigration practices and the militarization of the border between the United States and Mexico.[11] Cole (2014) suggests that Twitter might serve as an alternative venue for sharing writing, not in terms of marketing, but to create new forms of writing. In "Hafiz," Cole (2014) goes one step further, creating a collaborative Twitter essay that engages 31 people in 31 retweets. In this way, he experiments not only with writing but with the ways in which Twitter can be used in both the process of writing and the "publishing" or sharing of our products. Such experiments embrace the performative, unfinished nature and the collaborative process of the story form.

Lastly, I want to mention the possibilities for satire in ethnography. There are increasingly great examples of the use of satire, humor, and comedy in cultural and political critiques. For instance, Howard Campbell (2006) uses a satirical story of Chona, a Mexican-American graduate student, to reflect on the politics of the American Anthropology Association's annual conference. Feminist geographer Heather McLean similarly pokes fun at the elitism and sexism in the academy and the commodification of knowledge with a satirical performance of hipster academic "Toby Smart."[12] John Jackson, Jr. (2005) evokes Anthroman as a "kind of ethnographic hero" who helps him methodologically work through the field site and the ethics of asking strangers to tell private stories about their lives. Briony Lipton (2014) considers the history of Aboriginal women and the politics of whiteness in Australia through a counter-narrative that subverts the Cinderella story. All are cleverly crafted, unexpected stories, grounded in social and ethnographic research and experience, which offer opportunities to address the sorts of issues that anthropological discourse does not always make possible. Satire is also an effective way to make obvious the ways in which power insidiously works through normative and hegemonic structures or institutions like the academy, medicine, discourse, and the state.[13]

Writing Content Imaginatively

I dream of a writing that would be neither philosophy nor literature,
nor even contaminated by one of the other, while still keeping—
I have no desire to abandon this—the memory of literature and
philosophy.

—Jacques Derrida (1992, 73)

After this exploration of new forms—poetry, drawing, and micro-essays—I turn to experiments in writing that focus more on content, or what we write about. I advocate here for two types of ethnographic writing: (1) what Ann Cvetkovich (2012) has called "process-based writing," and (2) writing that is informed by an attention to embodiment and the senses in research.

Process-Based Writing

By "writing imaginatively," I mean using the imagination to write about the unexpected, the idiosyncratic, the sensorial, the everyday—all the sorts of things we often ignore in our writing.[14] One way to get at those sorts of everyday phenomena is to think about the ways in which writing is embodied and performative, or in other words, to focus on the corporeal performance of writing, and to be attuned to the process and the act of writing.

Cultural studies scholar Ann Cvetkovich (2012) has mapped out an approach to writing that she calls "process-based writing." As she explains, attention

IMAGE 2.2: Writing and research, Corinna Gurney, Vancouver, Canada.

Credit: AHAH Project, 2006.

to "sensation, tactility, and feelings," and to the social, cultural, and historical contexts of where and how these arise, makes space for "new forms of documentation and writing" (Cvetkovich 2012, 11). Reflecting on her own decision to use memoir to write about depression as a social and political phenomenon, Cvetkovich explains that the craft of writing is a way to "open up," to allow for speculative thinking, unfinished thoughts, and imagination to enter our writing. She argues that this allows for unexpected, peripheral, and unorthodox ideas and connections to emerge, resulting in creative accounts of social and political life. Process-based writing can also free the writer to challenge disciplinary and institutional regimes of writing, which can constrain or even prevent us from telling the types of stories that matter to our interlocutors and that have transformative potential to unsettle; it undisciplines our writing. Her approach is consistent with the notion that we must retrain ourselves to see the world if we are to draw it or write poetically about it. It involves slowing things down, cultivating a careful awareness and attention to both minutia and larger forces of power, and nurturing a sensitivity to seeing, knowing, and representing the intimacies and rhythms of lives that sometimes slip by in everyday moments of chaos.

Such an approach is consistent with the tradition of performative and embodied writing that "welcomes the body in to the mind's dwelling" (Pelias 2005, 417;

Madison 1999; see also Magdalena Kazubowski-Houston's chapter, "Performing," in this volume). Process-based writing also encourages partial, fragmented stories and acknowledges unfinished products as being representative of life itself (Clifford 1986). Such writing challenges neoliberal, conservative, colonial, and academic structures that impose particular logics on and of knowledge. Cvetkovich (2012, 23) also argues for shifting the essay form to a "public genre for speculative thinking." In doing so, she explains, she is "inspired by the desire to craft new forms of writing and knowledge that come from affective experience, ordinary life, and alternative archives" (23). Her book *Depression: A Public Feeling* bridges cultural analysis, memoir, and ethnography to offer a raw and unedited account of her struggle with mental health issues which disrupts and disturbs. Such imaginative practices assume "a commitment to openness" in inquiry.

Embodiment and the Senses

That openness in writing of which Cvetkovich speaks partly involves attending to sensorial experience and ways of knowing (see Dara Culhane's chapter, "Sensing," in this volume). Two ethnographies offer surprising provocations for those of us writing in anthropology because of their attention to the sensorial character of the field and the embodied nature of writing itself: Michael Taussig's *My Cocaine Museum* (2004) and Kathleen Stewart's *Ordinary Affects* (2007). What I admire about these two works is that they pay particular attention to sensations (color, taste, feeling, seeing) and the mundane. In *My Cocaine Museum*, Taussig (2004, 29) describes for us the colors of gold and how such colors come "out of blackness" and the feeling of heat and rain in the tropics of Colombia. He evokes the sensory experience of ordinary everyday life as profoundly as its striking, extraordinary violence. This ethnography is so rich in its attention to the sensorial realm that one can almost smell the "dank forests," taste the bitterness, touch the lover, and feel the water rush over oneself. But doing so does not sacrifice a deeply theoretical analysis: the colors of gold only make sense in relation to their dark histories of violence and accumulation. The ethnographic stories theorize colonialism, capitalist logics, and state violence while being attuned to the sensorial of everyday life in the tropics.

Stewart's *Ordinary Affects* (2007, 71) is exemplary for the attention to "the textures and rhythms of forms of living as they are being composed and suffered in social and cultural poesis." She takes seriously the mundane, quotidian aspects of life in a series of scenes that speak to the ways in which sensations and emotions shape and bring meaning to our lives. Describing American motels, shopping malls, and casinos, she evokes the strange in the ordinary. It is a most unconventional ethnography and yet it does what ethnography promises to do—it captures real lives, lived as fragmentary, partial, incomplete moments. Although written in prose, it is compellingly poetic. Stewart avoids overt theorization of these moments and lives, instead allowing the stories, as "felt theories" (Million 2014), to impress upon the reader.

Hugh Raffles's *Insectopedia* (2011) and Michael Jackson's *In Sierra Leone* (2004) are two very different models of ethnographies that take up history, literature, and philosophy as integral to the ethnographic stories they are telling. Like Taussig and Stewart, both authors challenge the traditions of ethnography and representation by writing ethnographies that capture parts of life that seem insignificant but yet are representative of lives everywhere because of the shared forces that shape, contort, and constrain. *Insectopedia*, a history and ethnography of flies, cockroaches, and other bugs, is a series of 26 essays that capture the essence of insects and their agency in our world. Like Stewart's *Ordinary Affects*, the individual stories do not necessarily need to be read in order. They stand on their own, even though they are intimately connected. It also favors a "weak theory" approach, one that pays more attention to objects and the senses (arousal, fear, smells) than grand narrative. And yet, it speaks critically to global forces and violence seen in the Holocaust, Chernobyl, and climate change. It moves temporally and spatially, eschewing linear thought. Based on multisited fieldwork in India, China, and New Mexico, it brings art, literature, science, history, and ethnography into one narrative. And importantly, it is written in a way that appeals to many audiences, not only academics.

In Sierra Leone is a very different ethnography (Jackson 2004). It is part memoir, part literary narrative, part ethnography, part history. It weaves together multiple, interconnected stories: the anthropologist/narrator Jackson; his informant Sewa Bockarie Marah (S.B.), of whom he has promised to write a biography; and the intimate history of a landscape and peoples scarred by violence and civil wars. It is a sensuous read for its attention to the smallest details and for an honesty that is rare in contemporary anthropology. It is a delicately and carefully written narrative about individual lives and their lessons for our understanding of the human condition. Jackson substantively engages with both literature and philosophy, as a philosophical anthropologist who explores questions of hope, optimism, and reconciliation amidst suffering and poverty. His own memories and experiences of working in Sierra Leone for over 30 years are interwoven with literary references, the memoir accounts of S.B., and a historical account of the civil war. Like the other works here, this ethnography privileges what is sensed and what is felt, against the backdrop of historical, political, and social processes that shape our lives.

These ethnographers take mundane objects, spaces, and events that are often passed over, and then illuminate the hidden, taken-for-granted stories that lie within them. Imagine a pile of dirty dishes in a kitchen sink and unravel the hidden stories behind those dishes. For many of us, dirty dishes are just domestic work needing to be done, yet those dishes tell stories about the lives of others. An ethnographer who is attuned to his or her senses might perceive the stories that lie behind those dirty dishes. Does the room have a faint smell of leftover dinner from the night before, a smell of grease and stale coffee that lingers? Maybe the dishes tell a story of a tragic accident, a hurtful fight, too much drinking the night before. Of a broken plate, accidentally dropped or purposely thrown. Maybe they tell the story of ancient ceramics, or inherited porcelain from a *nonna*, or an artist's craft of hand painting. Maybe they tell a story of a single woman working three jobs to feed her kids with no time left to wash the dishes and a failing economic system that punishes the poor. Maybe the story is about the poisonous water that drips from the tap and the corporate cover-up of fracking. Or it is about depression and grief and their paralyzing effect on the will to get out of bed in the morning. Dirty dishes might tell any one of many complicated stories that we as anthropologists should be attuned to and that matter to the people with whom we conduct our research and the communities in which we work. Dishes are never just dishes.

Anthropologist as Writer/Artist/Creator/Poet/Blogger

All the works I have discussed embody the principles of imaginative ethnography as defined in our introduction. They share our commitment to experimenting with genres of style and form, an appreciation of the slow process of writing, an openness and honesty in their storytelling forms, and a concern with "affective modes of knowledge production" (Westmoreland 2011). Think about your own work in anthropology as a writer. Imagine your writing as being both research and documentation, method and theory, dialogue and monologue, poetry and prose, objective and subjective. An imaginative ethnography hopes to reinspire and reignite a form of ethnographic writing that challenges, opens up, disassembles, and shifts how we understand the social, political, economic, cultural, historical, and personal processes that shape and constrain our everyday lives. It sees the process of writing ethnography as an artistic, embodied practice as much as a form of academic "knowledge translation."

The ethnographies discussed here—from the poetic, to the graphic, to the sensorial—all merge art, critique, narrative, and theory. All are carefully created, whether composed, written, or drawn. In the film *Sunset Ethnography* (2014) Taussig and Muecke suggest that "experimental writing," like imaginative writing, demands that the writer let go of the process a little and let it be formed by the experiences, relationships, and the sensuousness of life. They suggest thinking not about writing *about* the world, but about writing *with* the world. The idea that writing is relational and collaborative, affective and effective, and creative and imaginative should guide our writing practice in whatever form it might take.

Student Exercises

1. The Canadian literary journal *Geist* has an annual "postcard" competition that could be an interesting practice for creating concise commentaries that combine images and narration. Find an old photograph from home and then create your own postcard. Write 500 words, fiction or nonfiction, about the image you have chosen. Create your own "postcard" using images or drawings from fieldwork, and then write a short ethnographic vignette that captures the image. See www.geist.com/contests/postcard-contest

2. Kirin Narayan's *Alive in the Writing* (2012) offers all kinds of short exercises, but my favorite asks you to describe, in two pages, an encounter from your research when your thinking was transformed by what you heard or observed.

3. Draw, doodle, or sketch out a scene from fieldwork or campus life.

4. Write an ethnographic haiku. From Japan originally, a haiku has 17 syllables in three lines, grouped as five, seven, five.

5. Play with form in your writing and create a writing collage. Write a short essay that includes an admixture of forms. For instance, begin with a poem, move into a visual essay using photographs, then a creative nonfiction story, and conclude with a montage of drawings, written words, images, and archived diary entries. The only rule: It must tell an ethnographic story.

6. Take one scene from your research or fieldwork experience and write three different stories about that one scene. Limit each story to 500 words.

Additional Resources

Websites

Renato Rosaldo, "How I Write"
> http://web.stanford.edu/group/howiwrite/Transcripts/Rosaldo_transcript.html

Durham University's Writing across Boundaries project, Writing on Writing: A series of short papers on writing by anthropologists such as Anna Tsing, Howard Becker, and Tim Ingold
> www.dur.ac.uk/writingacrossboundaries/writingonwriting

Lynda Barry's workshops
> http://thenearsightedmonkey.tumblr.com

Nick Sousanis's website, *Spin, Weave, and Cut*
> http://spinweaveandcut.com

Drawing Words and Writing Pictures
  http://dw-wp.com
Sunset Ethnography: A Film about Experimental Ethnography, with Stephen
  Muecke and Michael Taussig
  https://vimeo.com/113130961
Literary Experiments in Ethnography blog series, Centre for Imaginative
  Ethnography
  http://imaginativeethnography.org/imaginings/literary-experiments-in-
  ethnography
Drawings, Animations and Cartoons, Centre for Imaginative Ethnography:
  Resources for anthropologists interested in comics and animation
  http://imaginativeethnography.org/drawings
Laughing Matters, Centre for Imaginative Ethnography: Blog series
  that explores the use of satire, humor, and parody in cultural
  anthropology http://imaginativeethnography.org/imaginings/
  laughing-matters
Literature, Writing & Anthropology, *Cultural Anthropology*
  www.culanth.org/curated_collections/5-literature-writing-anthropology
Alan Klima's webpage on writing: Great for graduate students and faculty
  www.academicmuse.org
The Banff Centre, Literary Arts
  www.banffcentre.ca/literary-arts

Journals of Interest for Experimental Scholarly Writing

Creative Approaches to Research
  http://aqr.org.au/publications/creative-approaches-to-research
Anthropology and Humanism
  http://anthrosource.onlinelibrary.wiley.com/hub/journal/10.1111/
  (ISSN)1548-1409

References

Abu-Lughod, Lila. 1993. *Writing Women's Worlds: Bedouin Stories*. Berkeley: University of
  California.
Alcoff, Linda. 1991. "The Problem of Speaking for Others." *Cultural Critique* 20
  (Winter): 5–32.
Anzaldúa, Gloria. 1987. *Borderlands / La Frontera: The New Mestiza*. San Francisco: Aunt
  Jute Books.

Barry, Lynda. 2008. *What It Is*. Vancouver: Raincoast Books.

Bartoszko, Aleksandra, Annne Birgitte Leseth, and Marcin Ponomarew. 2010. *Public Space, Information Accessibility, Technology and Diversity at Oslo University College*. Oslo, Norway: Oslo University College.

Behar, Ruth. 1993. *Translated Woman: Crossing the Border with Esperanza's Story*. Boston: Beacon Press.

Behar, Ruth. 1996. *The Vulnerable Observer: Anthropology That Breaks Your Heart*. Boston: Beacon Press.

Behar, Ruth. 2007. "Ethnography in a Time of Blurred Genres." *Anthropology and Humanism* 32 (2): 145–55. http://dx.doi.org/10.1525/ahu.2007.32.2.145

Behar, Ruth, and Deborah Gordon, eds. 1995. *Women Writing Culture*. Berkeley: University of California Press.

Brown, Karen McCarthy. 2001. *Mama Lola: A Vodou Priestess in Brooklyn*. Berkeley: University of California Press.

Boyer, Dominic. 2016. "The Necessity of Being a Writer in Anthropology Today." In *The Anthropologist as Writer: Genres and Contexts in the Twenty-First Century*, ed. Helena Wulff, 21–32. New York: Berghahn.

Cahnmann-Taylor, Melisa. 2006. "Ghetto Teachers' Apology." *Anthropology and Humanism* 31 (1): 8.

Cahnmann-Taylor, Melisa. 2013. "A Taste of War, June 2006." *North Dakota Quarterly* 78 (2/3): 75.

Campbell, Howard. 2006. "At the Anthropology Meetings." *Qualitative Inquiry* 12 (1): 208–16. http://dx.doi.org/10.1177/1077800405278753

Causey, Andrew. 2016. *Drawing to See: Drawing as an Ethnographic Method*. Toronto: University of Toronto Press.

Cole, Teju. 2014. "Teju Cole Writes a Story a Tweet at a Time." Interview by Michel Martin. NPR, 16 January. http://www.npr.org/2014/01/16/262473432/forget-the-new-yorker-storyteller-turns-to-twitter

Christian, Barbara. 1987. "The Race for Theory." *Cultural Critique* 6 (6): 51–63. http://dx.doi.org/10.2307/1354255

Clifford, James. 1986. "Introduction: Partial Truths." In *Writing Culture: The Poetics and Politics of Ethnography*, eds. James Clifford and George Marcus, 12–35. Berkeley: University of California Press.

Clifford, James, and George Marcus, eds. 1986. *Writing Culture: The Poetics and Politics of Ethnography*. Berkeley: University of California Press.

Cougnon, Louise-Amélie, and Cédrick Fairon, eds. 2014. *SMS Communication: A Linguistic Approach*. Amsterdam: John Benjamins. http://dx.doi.org/10.1075/bct.61

Cvetkovich, Anne. 2012. *Depression: A Public Feeling*. Durham, NC: Duke University Press. http://dx.doi.org/10.1215/9780822391852

Daniel, E. Valentine. 1996. *Charred Lullabies: Chapters in an Anthropology of Violence*. Princeton, NJ: Princeton University Press. http://dx.doi.org/10.1515/9781400822034

Daniel, E. Valentine. 2013. "The Coolie: An Unfinished Epic." In *Imperial Debris: On Ruins and Ruination*, ed. Ann Laura Stoler, 67–114. Durham, NC: Duke University Press. http://dx.doi.org/10.1215/9780822395850-003

Derrida, Jacques. 1992. "This Strange Institution Called Literature." In *Acts of Literature*, ed. D. Attridge, 33–75. London: Routledge.

Elliott, Denielle. 2014. "Truth, Shame, Complicity, and Flirtation: An Unconventional, Ethnographic (Non)fiction." *Anthropology and Humanism* 39 (2): 145–58. http://dx.doi.org/10.1111/anhu.12052

Elliott, Denielle. (Forthcoming). "The Problem with the Truth: Political Alliances, Pharmaceutical Science, and Storytelling in Nairobi." *Critical African Studies*.

Fassin, Didier. 2014. "True Life, Real Lives: Revisiting the Boundaries between Ethnography and Fiction." *American Ethnologist* 41 (1): 40–55. http://dx.doi.org/10.1111/amet.12059

Geertz, Clifford. 1989. *Work and Lives: The Anthropologist as Author*. Stanford, CA: Stanford University Press.

Gibb, Camilla. 2006. "Telling Tales out of School, a Research in Society Lecture Delivered at the 2007 Congress of the Humanities and Social Sciences." *ESC* 32 (2/3): 39–54.

Gordimer, Nadine. 1989. *The Essential Gesture: Writing, Politics and Places*. London: Penguin.

Hecht, Tobias. 2006. *After Life: An Ethnographic Novel*. Durham, NC: Duke University Press. http://dx.doi.org/10.1215/9780822387725

Hecht, Tobias. 2007. "A Case for Ethnographic Fiction." *Anthropology News* 48 (2): 17–18. http://dx.doi.org/10.1525/an.2007.48.2.17

Hendrickson, Carol. 2008. "Visual Field Notes: Drawing Insights in the Yucatan." *Visual Anthropology Review* 24 (2): 117–32. http://dx.doi.org/10.1111/j.1548-7458.2008.00009.x

Ingold, Tim. 2011. *Redrawing Anthropology: Materials, Movements, Lines*. Surrey, UK: Ashgate.

Jackson Jr., John. 2005. *Real Black: Adventures in Racial Sincerity*. Chicago: University of Chicago Press.

Jackson, Michael. 2004. *In Sierra Leone*. Durham, NC: Duke University Press. http://dx.doi.org/10.1215/9780822385561

Jackson, Michael. 2013. *The Other Shore: Essays on Writers and Writing*. Berkeley: University of California Press.

Johnson, Christopher. 2011. *Microstyle: The Art of Writing Little*. New York: Norton.

Kusserow, Adrie. 2002. *Hunting Down the Monk*. Rochester, NY: BOA Editions.

Kusserow, Adrie. 2014. *Refuge*. Rochester, NY: BOA Editions.

Langnes, L.L., and Geyla Frank. 1978. "Fact, Fiction, and the Ethnographic Novel." *Anthropology and Humanism* 3 (1–2): 18–22.

Lipton, Briony. 2014. "Cinderella, HerStory: An Alternate Pedagogical Approach to Aboriginal Women's History." *Creative Approaches to Research* 7 (2): 19–24.

Madison, Soyini. 1999. "Performing Theory/Embodied Writing." *Text and Performance Quarterly* 19 (2): 107–24. http://dx.doi.org/10.1080/10462939909366254

Maracle, Lee. 1996. *I Am Woman: A Native Perspective on Sociology and Feminism.* Vancouver: Press Gang.

Maynard, Kent. 2001. *Sunk Like God behind the House.* Kent, OH: Kent State University Press.

Maynard, Kent. 2002. "An 'Imagination of Order': The Suspicion of Structure in Anthropology and Poetry." *Antioch Review* 60 (2): 220–43. http://dx.doi.org/10.2307/4614312

Maynard, Kent. 2009. "Rhyme and Reasons: The Epistemology of Ethnographic Poetry." *Etnofoor* 21 (2): 115–29.

Maynard, Kent, and Melisa Cahnmann-Taylor. 2010. "Anthropology at the Edge of Words: Where Poetry and Ethnography Meet." *Anthropology and Humanism* 35 (1): 2–19. http://dx.doi.org/10.1111/j.1548-1409.2010.01049.x

McLean, Stuart. 2009. "Stories and Cosmogonies: Imagining Creativity Beyond 'Nature' and 'Culture.'" *Cultural Anthropology* 24 (2): 213–45. http://dx.doi.org/10.1111/j.1548-1360.2009.01130.x

McLean, Stuart. Forthcoming. "Sea." In *Writing Ethnography*, eds. Stuart McLean and Ananda Pandian. Santa Fe, NM: SAR.

Million, Dian. 2011. "Intense Dreaming: Theories, Narratives, and Our Search for Home." *American Indian Quarterly* 35 (3): 313–33. http://dx.doi.org/10.5250/amerindiquar.35.3.0313

Million, Dian. 2014. "There Is a River in Me: Theory from Life." In *Theorizing Native Studies*, eds. Audra Simpson and Andrea Smith, 31–42. Durham, NC: Duke University Press. http://dx.doi.org/10.1215/9780822376613-002

Mittermaier, Amira. 2011. *Dreams That Matter: Egyptian Landscapes of the Imagination.* Berkeley: University of California Press.

Narayan, Kirin. 1999. "Ethnography and Fiction: Where Is the Border?" *Anthropology and Humanism* 24 (2): 134–47. http://dx.doi.org/10.1525/ahu.1999.24.2.134

Narayan, Kirin. 2007. "Tools to Shape Texts: What Creative Nonfiction Can Offer Ethnography." *Anthropology and Humanism* 32 (2): 130–44. http://dx.doi.org/10.1525/ahu.2007.32.2.130

Narayan, Kirin. 2012. *Alive in the Writing: Crafting Ethnography in the Company of Chekhov.* Chicago: University of Chicago Press. http://dx.doi.org/10.7208/chicago/9780226567921.001.0001

Pandian, Anand, and M.P. Mariappan. 2014. *Ayya's Account: A Ledger of Hope in Modern India.* Bloomington: Indiana University Press.

Pandolfo, Stefania. 1997. *Impasse of the Angels: Scenes from a Moroccan Space of Memory.* Berkeley: University of California Press.

Pelias, Ronald. 2005. "Performative Writing as Scholarship: An Apology, an Argument, an Anecdote." *Cultural Studies, Critical Methodologies* 5 (4): 415–24. http://dx.doi.org/ 10.1177/1532708605279694

Pollock, Della. 1998. "Performative Writing." In *The Ends of Performance*, eds. Peggy Phelan and Jill Lane, 73–103. New York: NYU Press.

Raffles, Hugh. 2011. *Insectopedia*. New York: Vintage Press.

Rajabali, Anar. 2014. "On Writing A Poem: A Phenomenological Inquiry." *Creative Approaches to Research* 7 (2): 39–50.

Rosaldo, Renato. 2013. *The Day of Shelly's Death: The Poetry and Ethnography of Grief.* Durham, NC: Duke University Press. http://dx.doi.org/10.1215/9780822376736

Rothman, Joshua. 2014. "Why Is Academic Writing So Academic?" *New Yorker,* 20 February. http://www.newyorker.com/books/page-turner/why-is-academic-writing-so-academic

Shostak, Marjorie. 1981. *Nisa: The Life and Words of a !Kung Woman.* Cambridge, MA: Harvard University Press.

Simpson, Audra, and Andrea Smith, eds. 2014. *Theorizing Native Studies.* Durham, NC: Duke University Press. http://dx.doi.org/10.1215/9780822376613

Sousanis, Nick. 2015. *Unflattening.* Cambridge, MA: Harvard University Press.

Stoller, Paul. 1994. "Ethnographies as Texts/Ethnographers as Griots." *American Ethnologist* 21 (2): 353–66. http://dx.doi.org/10.1525/ae.1994.21.2.02a00070

Stoller, Paul. 2005. *Stranger in the Village of the Sick: A Memoir of Cancer, Sorcery, and Healing.* Boston: Beacon Press.

Stewart, Kathleen. 2007. *Ordinary Affects.* Durham, NC: Duke University Press. http://dx.doi.org/10.1215/9780822390404

Stommel, Jesse. 2012. "The Twitter Essay." *Hybrid Pedagogy: A Digital Journal of Learning, Teaching, and Technology.* http://www.digitalpedagogylab.com/hybridped/the-twitter-essay

Taussig, Michael. 2004. *My Cocaine Museum.* Chicago: University of Chicago Press. http://dx.doi.org/10.7208/chicago/9780226790152.001.0001

Taussig, Michael. 2011. *I Swear I Saw This: Drawings in Fieldwork Notebooks, Namely My Own.* Chicago: University of Chicago Press. http://dx.doi.org/10.7208/chicago/9780226789842.001.0001

Taylor, Jessica. 2012. "The Lines Between: Relational Subjectivities and the Practice of Observational Drawing." *Anthropology News* 14(1). http://www.anthropologymatters.com/index.php/anth_matters/article/view/271/449

Wainaina, Binyavanga. 2011. *One Day I Will Write about This Place.* Minneapolis: Graywolf Press.

Westmoreland, Mark. 2011. "Ethnography + Art: Convergence or Collision?" *IBRAAZ,* 1 June, http://www.ibraaz.org/essays/11

Wulff, Helena, ed. 2016. *The Anthropologist as Writer: Genres and Contexts in the Twenty-First Century.* New York: Berghahn.

Notes

1   See http://africasacountry.com/2014/01/watch-binyavangas-brilliant-youtube-documentary-when-you-look-at-the-map-of-gay-rights-around-the-world-why-is-ours-bright-red, accessed 9 March 2015.

2   Following Narayan (2007, 135), I define ethnography as "a practice of writing about people that is explicitly rooted in fieldwork and which originated in the discipline of anthropology."

3   Some key essays in these debates include those by Behar (2007); Clifford and Marcus (1986); Fassin (2014); Gibb (2006); Narayan (1999, 2007); Langnes and Frank (1978); and Stoller (1994).

4   See her webpage for a full list of her poetry publications, https://teachersactup.com

5   Daniel's ethnography, *Charred Lullabies: Chapters in an Anthropology of Violence* (1996) is another example of an ethnography that pushes the boundaries of traditional writing.

6   Also called an "alexandrine," this form includes a line with twelve syllables and six iambs (unstressed syllable followed by a stressed syllable).

7   For more on graphic novels see the University of Toronto Press's blog series on graphic novels, "Graphic Adventures in Anthropology," at www.utpteachingculture.com/announcing-ethnographic-a-new-series

8   From his interview for the graphic novel series with University of Toronto Press at www.utpteachingculture.com/unflattening-scholarship-with-comics

9   See her webpage, http://jilltxt.net/?p=15

10   See the National Public Radio interview with Teju Cole on his use of Twitter in his writing and politics at www.npr.org/2014/01/16/262473432/forget-the-new-yorker-storyteller-turns-to-twitter

11   See "A Piece of the Wall" at https://twitter.com/apieceofthewall

12   Watch the video performance at http://antipodefoundation.org/2013/03/28/featured-video-a-buzz-in-my-hub

13   For instance, see the satirical spoof "Radi-Aid," by Africans for Norway, which mocks the BandAid humanitarian initiatives that stereotype all Africans as poor and in need. In Radi-Aid, South Africans collect radiators to send to Norwegians who are dying from the cold. See it at www.rustyradiator.com

14   For writing about the imagination or dreams, in contrast, see Mittermaier (2011) or Pandolfo (1997).

CHAPTER 3

SENSING

Dara Culhane

IMAGE 3.1: "The Creator," artist Anna Waschke of Wandering Star Studio, Alaska.

Credit: Dara Culhane, 2016.

And so sensuous scholarship is ultimately a mixing of head and heart.
It is an opening of one's being to the world—a welcoming.
                    —Paul Stoller, Sensuous Scholarship *(1997, xviii)*

Welcome to a sojourn into sensory ethnography! The key questions animating our inquiry will be, What is sensory ethnography? How is it practiced? What contributions may sensory ethnography make to *A Different Kind of Ethnography*?

What Is *Sensory* Ethnography?

In her 2015 edition of *Doing Sensory Ethnography*, Sarah Pink notes that sensory experiences, like imagination and creativity, are integral to human social relations. "The experiencing, knowing body is central to the idea of a sensory ethnography," she writes (Pink 2015, 28). Take a moment to think about this. The premises of sensory ethnography are quite straightforward: humans are embodied, multisensory beings. We experience ourselves, each other, and nonhumans through what Ingold (2011a) calls our "entanglements" with the world: the interrelationships among embodiment, affect, imagination, and sensory experience, shot through by power and history. Sensory ethnography considers such emplaced, lived experience as integral to ways of knowing and feeling and to co-creating knowledge (Porcello et al. 2010). We come to know ourselves and each other through multiple avenues, including cultural traditions, political/economic relations, familial and individual biographies, and sensory experience and communication. "How people look, talk, sound, smell or touch can influence whether they are stigmatized or treated with respect, and whether they are identified with one social group, community, and class or another" (Robben 2008, 388). Understood this way, why ethnographers should be interested in sensory studies seems obvious. Sensory ethnography offers to enrich our understandings of diverse ways of knowing and being in the world and is therefore vital to ethnography.

This chapter is organized around a series of exercises interwoven with discussions about sensory ethnography as this field has emerged within contemporary anthropology. The exercises are designed to help you learn how to pay close attention to sensory experiences and processes of sensory knowledge co-creation, to reflect on how these may be culturally specific and politically consequential, and to begin integrating practices of "sensory embodied reflexivity" into your own research practices.

Conventionally, ethnographers privilege how people share knowledge through speaking and/or writing words, and communicate their research in written texts published by academic houses and in lecture halls to academic audiences. Increasingly, contemporary ethnographers seek to present our research in other formats as well. We create photographic collections, make films or sound recordings, mount installations and museum exhibits, and develop live performances. As anthropologist Michael Herzfeld writes, "It is a matter of political as well as epistemological urgency for the discipline to become much more sensitive to the messages couched in alternative sensory codes.... The older mode of sense-less description indeed now begins to smell rather fishy" (2008, 437, 441).

What Is Sensory *Knowledge?*

In the existing literature on sensory ethnography, one encounters repetitions of certain adjectives. Sensory knowledge is "non-verbal," "tacit," "taken for granted," "felt," "performed," "invisible," "emotional," "mundane," "intuitive," "emplaced," "imagined." Sensory knowledge is "not easily or even possibly expressed in written or spoken words" (Pink 2015, 164). Ethnographers are challenged to understand how experiencing, knowing, feeling bodies are engaged in diverse ways of knowing, what we call epistemologies. What do experiencing, feeling bodies know? And how do we come to know what our bodies know?

Sensory ethnography includes experiences and knowledge that may not be expressible in words. This may appear an irresolvable conundrum, at least in theory. What if we turn to practice, to what some sensory ethnographers *do?* How do they communicate what may be inexpressible in language? The venerable anthropologist Margaret Mead describes anthropology, critically, as a "discipline of words" (Mead [1974] 2003, 4). Bateson and Mead's 1942 publication *Balinese Character* advances arguments for recognizing photography as both a viable and a necessary ethnographic method for learning and understanding the centrality of the visual and of embodied learning, core features of Balinese culture not revealed through conventional observation and interviewing. Bateson and Mead used images primarily to document and represent observations made during fieldwork, and their work became a foundational text in the field of visual anthropology most closely associated with the documentary film tradition. French anthropologist and filmmaker Jean Rouch inaugurated another lineage in visual anthropology infused by creative challenges to documentary realism, interests in performance and theatre, and a critique of ethnography as a detached activity resulting in descriptive, observational reports. Rouch engaged African collaborators in filming rituals performed as anticolonial critique (Rouch, *Les Maîtres Fous*, 1955). He conducted what we might now call "anthropology at home" in a reflexive film about French intellectuals and artists (Rouch, *Chronicle d'un été* [co-directed by Edgar Morin], 1960) and "reverse anthropology" in a short film where a group of young Nigerian men narrate their visit to Paris in a work of political satire (Rouch, *Petit à Petit*, 1970; see also Stoller, 1992).

While visual anthropology has historically dominated nontextual or extra-textual ethnography, sensory ethnography is interested in the multisensory or polysensory nature of lived experience. Steven Feld, for example, began his career as an ethnomusicologist in the 1970s working with Kaluli people in Papua New Guinea (Feld 1982). They taught him about interrelationships among the sounds of women weeping, birds singing, and rain falling, and their imbrication in everyday life in a rain forest (Feld 1982; Feld and Brenneis 2004). Feld describes his contemporary work as "acoustemology," a portmanteau word for "acoustic epistemology." He writes, "These days I am exploring acoustic knowing as a centrepiece of Kaluli experience; how sounding and the sensual, bodily, experiencing of sound is a special kind of knowing" (Feld 1994, 10). Feld and other sound ethnographers make their work available in multiple audio and audiovisual formats. (See Boudreault-Fournier, Chapter 4, in this volume.)

Paul Stoller (1989) describes how his understanding of sensory epistemologies changed when he became an apprentice to a shaman. Songhay shamans in Niger, who taught him about their healing practices, consider the stomach the site of personality and agency. As they believe that knowledge emerges through a process of ingestion, their stomachs, he writes, allow them to "eat power and history" (5). His fieldwork has taught him "epistemological humility": "One cannot separate thought from feeling and action. . . . Now I let the sights, sounds, smells and tastes of Niger flow into me. This fundamental rule in epistemological humility taught me that taste, smell, and hearing are often more important for the Songhay than sight, the privileged sense of the West. In Songhay one can taste kinship, smell witches, and hear the ancestors" (5).[1] Anthropologist Andrew Irving studies relationships between sensory experience and urban space. He invites pedestrians to record streams of consciousness, or interior monologues, as they walk through specific areas of the city. Irving found that walking across *bridges*, suspended between land, water, and air, "established a new sense of scale against which citizens could compare their finite, organic bodies" (2013, 290).[2]

Relationships to illness and healing have made sensory ethnography and knowledge of continuing interest to medical anthropology. Participating in public debates in the Netherlands about when and how doctors could determine that an Alzheimer's patient's refusal of food was a signal of their desire to end their life, Hans Harbers and his colleagues (2002, 207) set out "to intervene in the deadlocked relation between biomedicine and ethics with the taste of chocolate as a lever." Considering the case of a woman who began refusing any food that did not taste like chocolate, and then would eat only a specific brand brought to her by her son when he visited, Harbers and colleagues ask how this story might aid in developing ethical policies about end-of-life care. They argue that sensory experiences like taste and ingestion are connected in lived experience to memory, intimate relations, and love, and should be understood as vital to social relations. They advocate for ethnographic research into the lived, sensory experiences not only of terminally ill patients and their families but also of daily care providers like kitchen staff and nursing assistants, to inform policy on euthanasia.

These examples show that sensory ethnography begins with multisensory experience. Each element in this description is important and distinct. Let's delve in and get a better understanding by using our own senses.

What Is Multisensory, Embodied, Affective, Lived Experience?

Cultivating a Sensory Embodied Reflexivity

Performance ethnographer Dwight Conquergood (1991, 180) argues, "Ethnography is an *embodied practice*; it is an intensely sensuous way of knowing. The embodied researcher is the instrument." To become critically aware of our own sensory experiences, the meanings we make of these, and how we apply them is challenging and requires purposeful work that begins with cultivating "sensory embodied reflexivity." (See also Katzman 2015; Pink 2015.) This starts with learning to pay close attention to sensory experiences.

The exercises in this chapter are designed as imaginative practices—invitations to experiment, play, reflect, and question. Like all pedagogical strategies, these exercises involve interrelated processes of unlearning and learning, of becoming conscious of deeply sedimented ways of experiencing and interpreting sensation, of learning about other ways of doing so, and of considering the senses as arenas of agency, sites where you experience and *act*. Each exercise may be carried out by one person, in pairs, or in groups. In the pages that follow, you are invited to tack back and forth between doing exercises, reading the text, and recording and critically reflecting on your experiences and analyses.

Here are a few basic instructions to guide you through each exercise. The exercises ask you to engage in free-writing, free-speaking, free-drawing, and free-moving. If the task has a specific time limit, set your timer and when it starts, begin writing or drawing or speaking or moving and continue doing so until the alarm rings. If only one word or a string of words, or sounds, or only penciled scribbles come to you, simply repeat until the alarm sounds. It is important to keep going for the full duration of the time limit.

The main points to remember are (1) you are both creator and audience; (2) you are engaged in an experiment, and the outcomes are unknown; and (3) if you are doing this by yourself, no one will see or hear or read your records of the exercises without your consent. If you are doing them with others, you will negotiate how to share your reflections. The important thing to remember is that these exercises are open-ended self-explorations. There is no buried treasure of correct answers awaiting discovery.

Preparations for each exercise:

- Step 1:
  Take a few minutes to settle into your work space.
  Take a deep breath or two or three.
- Step 2:
  Read over the exercise directions.
  Take a deep breath or two or three.
- Step 3:
  Choose how you will record your responses so you can reflect on them and share them with others later if you so choose. You may write, draw or paint, speak, sing, or dance, and record, play it back, watch, or listen.
  Take a deep breath or two or three.

It is time for the first exercise. We begin with writing, text being the medium we are most familiar with in academic work.

Exercise 1: The Basics of Sensing—Right Here, Write Now

Set your timer for five minutes, and spend one minute on each task set out below.

- Write down what you are seeing.
- Write down what you are hearing.
- Write down what you are smelling.
- Write down what you are tasting.
- Write down what you are touching.

The goal of this exercise is to pay close attention to how you experience a moment in time and place with five senses.

Try variations on this exercise: Close your eyes and/or plug your ears and/or hold your nose when you concentrate on other senses. What difference does it make to your sensory experiences when you do this?

Multisensory

Smelling the aroma of a particular food may evoke memories and associations of sights, sounds, tastes, touches, people, and stories from other times and other places. We may recall hearing someone's words—perhaps kind, perhaps cruel—and this in turn may provoke feelings of affection or fear, loss or yearning. Remembering prompts our present bodies/minds/feelings to imagine and respond to future encounters. Our "hearts race," our "jaws drop," our "stomachs clench," our "skin crawls," our "spirits lift," or our "dreams shatter" when an image flashes in our imagination. Feeling "butterflies" in our stomachs may be a sign that we are experiencing sensations/thoughts/feelings. In all these ways, our senses "speak," making themselves known to us through processes that simultaneously engage our bodies/minds/feelings.

John Hockey and Jacquelyn Allen-Collinson (2009, 226) call for attention to the sensory experiences of bodies at work, to the "smell (and sensations) of sweat on skin ... [that] ... testifies that the body is engaged in demanding labour." The presence of and responses to scents can also be bound up in social tensions, as Martin Manalansan (2006) discusses in his work on "the politics of olfaction"; for example, cooking smells can be the site of conflict between "hosts" and "immigrants." What does your body smell like at work? What are the sensory skills required in your life? Are there alliances and/or conflicts in your life that revolve around sensory experience?

Although scientists now estimate that there are at least 10 senses, and perhaps as many as 33, Western philosophy and social theory conventionally select to focus on only five senses, understood to be separate from each other, with sight prized most of all, followed by hearing (Howes 2009, 22–25). The layout of Exercise 1, which you just completed, reflects this culturally and historically specific formulation of only five distinct senses. Is this familiar to you? Strange?

Anthropology and the Senses

Although social scientists, writers, and artists have long been interested in the senses, work initiated by anthropologist David Howes, cultural historian Constance Classen, and sociologist Richard Synnott at Concordia University in Montreal, Quebec, marks the emergence of the distinct field called the "anthropology of the senses" (Classen, Howes, and Synnott, 1994; Classen 1998, 2012; Howes 1991, 2004, 2013; Howes and Classen 2014). Through comparative cultural and historical research, their work critiques the universalizing assumptions of Western sensory theory. They demonstrate the tremendous diversity within and between cultures and over time, documenting how many and which senses people recognize, whether or not they understand senses hierarchically, and how relationships among senses and cultural/political/cosmological contexts are analyzed. Classen, Howes, and Synnott also criticize the "verbocentric" and "textcentric" academic traditions that mitigate against recognizing forms of sensory knowledge that resist representation by the written word. Sharing this focus, the Sensory Ethnography Laboratory (SEL) at Harvard University is dedicated to ethnographic filmmaking. Its mission is described as encouraging "attention to the many dimensions of the world, both animate and inanimate, that may only with difficulty, if it all, be rendered with propositional prose" (Sensory Ethnography Lab, n.d.).

Anthropologist Tim Ingold (2011b) argues that Howes and his colleagues impose an abstract and overly homogenizing concept of "culture" onto lived experience (see also Howes 2010, 2011; Pink 2010 for further insight into these debates). In the contemporary world people move more and more frequently through multiple geopolitical landscapes, commonly consume, for example, what Arjun Appadurai (1990) calls the products of transnational "mediascapes," and form complex communities where *inter-* and *intra*-cultural diversity demands attention. Ingold's critique reflects contemporary debates in anthropology about whether the discipline's conventional concept of "culture" tied to nation-state borders is productive (Abu-Lughod 1991; Gupta and Ferguson 1997).

That media and the creative arts may engage sensory experiences that are difficult or impossible to express in words is undeniable. However, Ingold (2011b) cautions against too quickly dismissing the possibilities of written expression and notes the dangers of simply replacing the dominance of the word with that of the image. Many contemporary ethnographers are exploring what writing can do by experimenting with different genres (see, for example, Denielle Elliott's chapter, "Writing," in this volume, and Elliott 2014). Examples abound: Renato Rosaldo works in ethnographic poetry (2013), and perfor-mance ethnographer D. Soyini Madison (2011, 181–99) advocates the practice of "performative ethnographic writing" that is evocative, embodied, relational, and consequential. Intense affective/political experiences in the United States infuse Kathleen Stewart's (2007) written storytelling. In addition to his work on shamanic healing in West Africa (1989), Paul Stoller wrote about street vending in New York City (2002) and has authored fiction inspired by ethnographic research (1999). Like imagination that resists abstract theoretical confinement, ethnographic attention to sensory experience invites us to re-imagine our minds and bodies, ideas and feelings, not as binaries that are separate from and opposed to each other but rather as actively living in perpetual and dynamic interaction with each other.

Exercise 2: Walking and Chewing Gum at the Same Time, or Sensory Mashup
Return to Exercise 1. Select two or more senses that you will pay attention to simultaneously. For example, while you are smelling, what are you tasting?

While you are listening, what are you touching? Do three pairs of senses for two minutes each, and write down your responses.

Challenging, right? The first goal of this exercise is to notice the connections between senses and the tensions between theory and experience. If you focused your attention on seeing, for example, you were simultaneously experiencing hearing. Did sound seem to shift to the background of your attention? When you wrote down your experiences, did you use typical academic language or describe your experiences chronologically? The second goal of this exercise is to engage with questions about the possibilities of communicating sensory experience in experimental textual forms. Poetry, for example, breaks away from formal writing rules and chronology. Try writing and reading your responses as poems. What do you notice?

Embodied

Theories advancing ways of understanding the body's relevance to social theory are many, and are currently the subject of lively debate (for a comprehensive overview, see Mascia-Lees 2011). Central, enduring conversations focus on relationships between the body theorized as text inscribed upon by society, and bodies theorized as agentive, inscribed upon and inscribing, entangled with society. Thomas Csordas's 1993 article "Somatic Modes of Attention" has been influential in sensory ethnography. He defines "somatic attention" as the "culturally elaborated ways of attending to and with one's body in surroundings that include the embodied presence of others" (138). Csordas thus draws on the work of philosopher Maurice Merleau-Ponty to set out a dynamic, relational theory of embodiment. Ingold (2011b) further argues that sensing bodies are not so much like texts inscribed by cultural/political contexts but are, rather, agentive and entangled with other human and nonhuman beings and our shared environments. The exercises in this chapter are informed by theoretical premises articulated by Csordas and Ingold, and invite you to undertake explorations in experiencing and reflecting on somatic modes of attention, necessarily emplaced and entangled with history, power, and social/cultural relations.

Affective

Dian Million (2013) uses the term "felt theory" to argue for the necessary and irreducible interrelationship between experience and theory that contemporary social theorists organize under the rubric of "affect." Writing about Indigenous women's literary autobiographies, Million (2013, 58) asks, "How is it that our voices, our oral traditions and our literary and historical voices, are suppressed by western knowledge that denies its own affective attachments to certain histories?" She then answers the question she poses: "Our voices rock the boat, and perhaps the world. Our voices are dangerous."

"Affect," as I use the term here, refers to feelings generated by—and, like embodiment, circulating through—relationships among people. Affect includes what we conventionally think of as discrete emotions like anger, fear, and love, but is not reducible to individualized emotional experience. Rather, affect is constituted by interconnected and energetic movements of feelings, circulating among people in particular places and times ("emplaced" beings).

Exercise 3: Polysensory—Tasting Touch, Smelling Sounds, Hearing Sights

In Exercises 1 and 2, did you struggle to express your sensory experiences in written words? Still, do you think you know what you saw, heard, smelled, tasted, or touched because you "felt it in your bones"? Did you wish you could use your hands to gesture when you were trying to describe what you were touching and how it felt? Or did you want to make facial expressions to communicate your experience of a smell? Could you draw what you saw? And how do we represent simultaneous sensory experiences? A central issue that brings ethnographers and artists into conversations about sensory ethnography revolves around the challenges these questions present. Text and image collage, montage, live performance, film, photography, music, and dance may facilitate the representation of overlapping, complex sensory experiences. The exercises invite you to take a first step in this direction by playing with a variety of modes of expression.

Repeat Exercise 1, but this time do so through free-drawing rather than writing. Use pencil or pen, crayons, markers, or paints. Free-draw, review, reflect, interrogate.

Repeat Exercise 1, but this time free-speak your responses. Audio-record them, listen, reflect, interrogate.

Repeat Exercise 1, but this time use free movement. Try facial expressions, gestures, and whole body movements. Video-record, watch, reflect, interrogate.

If you are doing this alone, stand in front of a mirror—be your own audience. If you are doing this with others, take turns being performer and audience. Have fun!

The goals of this exercise are first to experiment with nontextual forms of representation and communication of sensory experience and, second, to offer you bases for comparison with the results of Exercises 1 and 2.

Movement

Questions surrounding how movement participates in the co-creation of knowledge are addressed in exciting ways by dance ethnographers, who, as artist/scholars, struggle to integrate the embodied knowledge they hold in every fiber of their (dancing) beings with academic theorizing and to articulate sensory embodied epistemologies to diverse audiences (Barbour 2011;

Buckland 1999; Davida 2011). Such embodied knowledge emerges in political contexts and has implications, as seen in Aaron Glass's (2004) account of "underground dancing" among Kwakwaka'wakw First Nations in present-day British Columbia, Canada. Their dancing transmitted embodied knowledge to younger generations, in defiance of the Indian Act of Canada, which criminalized such cultural expression during the years 1885–1951.

Helena Wulff (2007) analyzes relationships among bodies, identities, and local/global economies in her study tracing traditional Irish dancing from rural crossroads to the transnational commercial success of *Riverdance*. Using the concept of a "sensory regime," Jennifer Roth-Gordon (2013) describes how young men in contemporary Brazil counter deeply classed, gendered, and racialized aesthetics by engaging in "politically conscious Hip Hop music." Karen Barbour (2012, 67), who explores sensory methodologies for auto-ethnographic performance, and who mixes movement exercises, images, creative writing, and academic analysis, writes: "Knowing arises through moving, not only through perception. We move to perceive and to understand. Movement itself is a way of knowing."

Exercise 4: Shake It All Up—Smelling Elbows and Hungry Toes

Return to Exercise 1. Set the timer for 10 minutes. Randomly assign imagined sensory capacities to body parts, moving your body accordingly, and recording your experience. What if your elbows could smell? (Take your elbow "nosing" around in your fridge.) What if your knees could listen? (Put your earphones on your knees and imagine they are listening to music.) What if your toes could taste, and your ears could type? Try it! Play! Have fun!

The purpose of this exercise is to use your imagination to "make the familiar strange," and builds on the movement exercise you completed in Exercise 3. Did imagining and moving your body in new ways surprise you with any insights into sensory experience? Humor and clowning are powerful tools that may offer critical insights into familiar ways of doing things. Write, dance, sing, draw your responses.

Intersubjectivity and Relationality

In a recent interview published online in the journal *Cultural Anthropology*, Thomas Csordas is asked about relationships among embodiment, affect, and political movements. He responds: "The first step toward understanding the political relevance of affect is to recognize that it is not just a locus of subjectivity but a feature of intersubjectivity. From there it's a short step to power, persuasion, and politics" (Csordas 2013).

Challenging social theories and popular thought that posit human society as being constituted by an aggregate of atomistic individuals, critical anthropologists hold that we humans are irreducibly social and relational beings who become selves in relationships with others. *Intersubjectivity* is the space of thinking/feeling/doing/being created by people interacting with each other in and through social relationships. It is more than the sum of its participants. It is the site where sensory ethnography is practiced. Exercises 1–4 invited you to practice in private if you chose to. Now, we are going out in public.

"To think with an enlarged mentality," Hannah Arendt (1989, 43) writes, "means that one trains one's imagination to go visiting."

Exercise 5: Take Your Sensory Imagination out Visiting

The goal of this exercise is to begin traveling through entanglements where sensory experience, autobiography, a moment in time and place, relations with others, and social theories meet.

Read, listen to, and watch your responses to Exercises 1-4. As you do so note the memories, stories, and associations with other people, times, places, thoughts, and feelings that your responses evoke as you review them. What bodily sensations accompany these experiences? Note whether some of your interpretations shift and change, and/or how others may remain the same. Pay close attention to your sensorial, embodied, affective experience. Does a particular memory fill you with dread? Do you feel that dread in your stomach? Does a story associated with food fill you with nostalgia? Where in your body do you feel what you name "nostalgia," and what does it feel like? Is this exercise "getting under your skin"? Experiment with different ways of expressing and reflecting on your sensory experiences. Write and read. Record and watch/listen. Draw, paint, dance. Watch yourself. Engage others in your exercises. Watch them.

The first goal of this exercise is to pay closer attention to how sensation registers in your body, to how you may communicate such embodied experience. The second goal reflects on how sensory experience is entangled in time and place and situation, and how interpretations and meanings may change. The third goal is to reflect on what this may suggest about relationships between sensory experience and sensory knowledge.

Phenomenology

Phenomenology figures prominently in theoretical formulations for understanding sensory ethnography. Unlike philosophical phenomenology, which is much criticized for assuming a disembodied, abstract relationship to the material world, anthropologists and ethnographers insist on close attention to life lived within entangled, intersubjective relationships. This commitment to lived experience characterizes sensory ethnography's conversations with phenomenology.

Desjarlais and Throop (2011, 87) describe phenomenological approaches as having "helped anthropologists to reconfigure what it means to be human, to have a body, to suffer and to heal, and to live among others." Learning to pay close attention to sensory experience is an ongoing process, and our skill in this regard is necessarily a work in progress.

Exercise 6: Self in the World, the World in the Self . . .

Imagine you live life entangled with multisensory environments. Tuck Exercise 1 into your pocket and take it out and about in the world with you. Notice how, when, why sensory experience and knowledge appears—and when you notice it. How do you know you feel like you "belong" (or do you?) when you walk the streets or trails or fields or beaches of spaces you call "home"? What does this feel like in your body? How do you know when, where, and why you "do not belong"? What does that feel like? To experience a sense of belonging to place, or, conversely, to feel oneself an excluded stranger involves complex entanglements among seeing, hearing, smelling, tasting, touching, imagining bodies, and environments.

When you watch films and listen to music, how do sensory experiences evoke embodied, affective responses? What are they and what do they feel like? Take some time to watch a film or listen to music. Record your responses: What do they feel like in your body? What ideas does this exercise evoke?

How do people you interact with talk about senses? Ask them. Have conversations about sensory experience. Tell them about the reading you are doing on sensory ethnography. Ask them what they think of these theories and research in sensory ethnography. Reflect on what they tell you. How do you and they communicate sensorally? Record reflections on this exercise. How do your conversations with people about the sensory agree with and/or challenge your reading here about sensory ethnography?

This exercise invites you to begin experimenting with questions about relationships among sensory experience, sensory knowledge, entanglements, and social theories.

Once again, consider the relationships between experience and theory: While we are paying close attention to our embodied sensory experience, we are likely not simultaneously, consciously, or purposefully analyzing our sociopolitical situation—our positionality within transnational neoliberal capitalism, for example, or our historical relationships with colonialism and empire. As ethnographers we take as given that we are necessarily positioned within these political formations. Sensory experience is a way of understanding these embodied entanglements.

History, Power, and Knowledge

Sensory Experience as Political Practice

"Our own sensory experience provides an essential basis for exploring ways of sensing," writes David Howes. "However, it is inadequate to rely solely on personal experience for understanding how people everywhere perceive the world. While humans share the same basic sensory capacities, these are developed and understood in different ways" (2013, 8–9).

Critical work begins by interrogating legacies that have created and defined the categories we are trained to think and work with. For sensory ethnographers this begins by taking analytic account of the limited conception of the senses within Western social theory, which conventionally recognizes only five (sight, sound, smell, taste, and touch), imagines them as distinct and separate from one another, orders them in a hierarchy, and believes this theoretical framework to sufficiently explain human experience across all places and times. In this canonical scheme, the "higher senses" of sight and sound are closely associated with the mind, and have been historically represented as most fully developed among elite Western European men. The "lower senses" of smell, taste, and touch have been most closely associated with body and the thoughts, feelings, and actions of Indigenous and other racialized "others," along with women, children, and the ill. Those whose imaginations have been represented as potentially destabilizing to the political order have been characterized as impelled by instincts and (animal) drives. "The reluctance of present-day anthropologists to examine or recognize the cultural importance of smell, taste, and touch is due not only to the relative marginalization of these senses in the modern West," anthropologist Michael Herzfeld writes, "but also to the racist tendencies of an earlier anthropology to associate the 'lower' senses with the 'lower' races" (2008, 436).

Recognizing this construction of the senses as particular to dominant theories in the West, we see that we live within sensory regimes, as Roth-Gordon (2013) terms it. Our bodies, feelings, imaginations, and senses are educated and trained in particular ways, and these are naturalized and considered "ordinary common sense." Practicing sensory ethnography leads us to question not only these dominant, entrenched ways of knowing and acting—but also those of conducting research. Consider the history of colonialism in Canada.

Seizure of Indigenous lands and resources is the driving force in colonial settlement in Canada as elsewhere, and Canadian state policy administered under the Indian Act of 1876 aimed at systematically severing Indigenous peoples' relationships with lands, resources, and kin, endeavoring to reconstruct Indigenous people "from the inside out" (Coulthard 2014; Simpson 2014; Simpson and Smith 2014; Million 2013). Spatial segregation on administered reserves, restrictions on mobility, intense surveillance of everyday private and public life, hospitalization and incarceration, and prohibition of cultural practices like potlatching—to name but a few strategies—directly targeted individual and collective Indigenous bodies, minds, thoughts, feelings, and sensations, penetrating and engineering everyday lived experience (Million 2013; Robertson and Kwaguł Gixsam Clan 2012). Colonial governance—clearly a "multisensory, embodied, and affective" program—was entrenched in the Indian residential school policy (1884–1996) that oversaw the removal of generations of children from their homes and kin to state- and church-run boarding schools. Beverley McLachlin, Chief Justice of the Supreme Court of Canada, recently named the policy a program of "cultural genocide" (Fine 2015).

Indigenous peoples' decolonization movements assert sovereignty over lands, resources, minds, bodies, feelings, memories, and imaginaries. Their struggles to reconstitute persons, families, collectivities, and nations make clear that sensory experience is both a site of colonizing governance and of decolonizing transformation. Indigenous history and contemporary movements reveal how deeply entangled sensory experience is with political power.

We have these sensory experiences in specific places, at particular times. What are the histories and political struggles that precede us, and how do we notice or not notice them with our senses? The method of "walking ethnography" has generated considerable interest among sensory ethnographers working on relationships with place (see, for example, Cristina Moretti's chapter, "Walking," in this volume, and Moretti 2015; Pink 2008).

Exercise 7: The Land beneath Your Feet

Choose a place that is significant to you for any reason. Before you set out, take five minutes to free-write, free-draw, free-speak, or free-move in response to the questions, What does this place mean to me? Why? and What do I imagine I will learn by taking a sensory walk here? Take these questions and Exercise 1, and some form of recording equipment (pencil and paper, camera, audio recorder) along with you on a sensory walk.

Consider the history of the place you are walking. For example, here in British Columbia, Canada, it has become the practice at public gatherings to recognize that Indigenous peoples are stewards of the lands on which the gathering is taking place. An organizer of an event might say, "We are meeting on the unceded territories of the Coast Salish First Nations and we wish to thank them for their hospitality." Such statements acknowledge both the long history of Indigenous life in this place and the relatively recent colonial settlement, and that Indigenous sovereignty and land rights continue to be contested in active political struggles today. What differences might it make to our sensory experience of walking when we pay close attention to the fact that the land upon which our feet are falling is Indigenous territory?

What is the history of the place where you are walking? Where did you learn about it? Or, do you know anything of this history? What difference does your own history, and/or your families' histories, make to your present experience and to your imagined futures in relation to this place? How is this experienced through your senses?

Intersubjectivity

Sensory ethnography not only privileges lived, embodied, and affective knowledge, but also focuses on intersubjectivity and the co-creation of such knowledge. Doing so raises critical epistemological questions about relationships between knowledge and power. Sensory knowledge co-creation is a process to which we bring our whole selves, and through which new ways of thinking/feeling emerge—shaped by, but not reducible to, traces of what each brings to the relationship. The relationship between intersubjectivity and sensory embodied reflexivity means that to know ourselves we must both practice introspective reflection and strive "to see ourselves as others see us." "Thus, it is a matter of political as well as epistemological urgency for the discipline to become much more sensitive to the messages couched in alternative sensory codes" (Herzfeld 2008, 437).

Political Sense

Multisensory, embodied, affective experiences and their significance for ethnographers have also been central to research and political movements in the work of feminist, queer, and radical scholars (Blackman 2009, 2011; Rooke 2009), and sensory ethnography draws upon their insights. Critical scholarship on embodiment, performance, and political economy is another stream within sensory ethnography. Alex Flynn and Jonas Tinius (2015) propose that Walter Benjamin's critique of commodification and its effect on social life and personhood offers a basis for a political anthropology of the senses (see also Howes 2005). Referencing the early twentieth-century Parisian arcades that served as prototypes of contemporary shopping malls, Benjamin (2002) describes the conflicting senses of alienation and attraction that he experiences when walking through an architectural space designed to generate desires to possess "things" that promise success and happiness. Benjamin experienced wandering the arcades as a dystopic commodification of everyday life, produced by industrial capitalism.

Exercise 8: Speaking of Capitalism

Take your sensory imagination for a walk in a shopping mall, or to a farmer's market, or to any other commercial site. Consider the site you visit a purposefully designed multisensory environment. You, the customer, are meant to take the sensory stimuli vendors offer into your minds/bodies, experience them, be changed to think/feel in specific ways, and become motivated to purchase and consume the products for sale.

Return to Exercise 1 and, for each sense, describe your experience in writing or drawing, or record your verbal commentary or how your body moves in response. Note what you imagine the vendors' intentions are with regard to what they hope to evoke in you. Consider the architecture of the space as a whole. Reflect on the fit and/or lack of fit between your experiences and your hypotheses about the designers' intentions. Do you want to buy anything? What? Why? Do you buy?

The purpose of this exercise is to experience a contemporary commercial sensory environment, to consider how your sensory experience is shaped in such an environment, and to imagine how you might exercise (sensory) agency in this context.

Using exercises to introduce you to sensory ethnography, I have sought to bring theory, experience, and pedagogy into conversation and into productive practice: to walk the talk, and to talk the walk. A first objective of the exercises is to invite you to begin paying close attention to sensory experience in a critical, purposeful way. For many of us, this may constitute a relatively new way of thinking/feeling/sensing, one that challenges us to further develop what I have been calling "sensory embodied reflexivity."

Sensory Embodied Reflexivity

Indigenous, feminist, and critical ethnographers in particular argue that political power relations infuse research and knowledge co-creation practices, and that we must therefore closely attend to relationships among ethnographers and research subjects, participants, and collaborators (Magnat 2011). A minimal expectation has become that ethnographers identify their positionality within structures of race, gender, class, sexuality, able-bodiedness, and local and extralocal geopolitics, with critical attention to both similarities and differences among themselves and people they are working with along these axes. Sensory ethnography, focused on where, when, and how people—in all their flesh and feelings—meet and experience the forces of, say, colonialism and racialization in their everyday lives, demands not only attention to such political positioning, but also that we, as ethnographers, come to know ourselves and others as multisensory, embodied beings engaged in co-creating knowledge.

But beyond self-realization, developing reflexive practices is crucial to sensory ethnographers' potential to engage in cultural and political critique. We live within sensory orders, and our bodies, feelings, imaginations, and senses are educated and trained in particular and diverse ways.

IMAGE 3.2: "Never Be Intimidated," Vancouver, Canada.

Credit: Dara Culhane, 2015.

Sensory ethnography asks how multisensory, embodied, affective, lived experience relates to epistemology (see Magnat 2011). What are the social and political processes through which ethnographic knowledge emerges? How do we know what we know?

Exercise 9: Epistemology: Feeling/ Knowing and Knowing/Feeling
Review your work on the exercises you have completed. Set the timer for 10 minutes and free-write, free-speak, free-draw, free-move in response to these questions: What difference does it make to me (citizen, student, person) to consider multisensory, embodied, affective, lived experience a valuable and legitimate basis of knowledge? Has working through this material changed my perspective on epistemology? On what constitutes ethnography?

Additional Resources

There is considerable, active conversation on the Web about sensory ethnography, sensory studies, arts, and sensory experience. Below is a small sample of key sites specifically associated with anthropology.

Websites

Centre for Imaginative Ethnography
www.imaginativeethnography.org
Centre for Sensory Studies, Concordia University
http://www.centreforsensorystudies.org
European Sensory Network
http://www.esn-network.com/research/
Sensory Ethnography Laboratory, Harvard University
http://sel.fas.harvard.edu/
http://vimeo.com/selab

Sensory Studies
www.sensorystudies.org/of-related-interest
Sound Studies Laboratory
www.soundstudieslab.org/projects/anthropology-of-sound
Studio for Ethnographic Design, University of California San Diego
https://quote.ucsd.edu/sed/tag/sensory-ethnography
Sensory Ethnography blog
http://monoskop.org/Sensory_ethnography

Journals

Sensate: A Journal for Experiments in Critical Media Practice
http://sensatejournal.com
The Senses and Society
www.tandfonline.com/loi/rfss20#.Vzj6zqukYXk

References

Abu-Lughod, Lila. 1991. "Writing against Culture." In *Recapturing Anthropology: Working in the Present*, ed. Richard G. Fox, 137–54. Santa Fe, NM: School of American Research Press.

Appadurai, Arjun. 1990. "Disjuncture and Difference in the Global Cultural Economy." *Public Culture* 2 (2): 1–24. http://dx.doi.org/10.1215/08992363-2-2-1

Arendt, Hannah. 1989. *Lectures on Kant's Political Philosophy*. Chicago: University of Chicago Press.

Barbour, Karen. 2011. *Dancing across the Page: Narrative and Embodied Ways of Knowing*. Chicago: University of Chicago Press.

Barbour, Karen. 2012. "Standing Center: Autoethnographic Writing and Solo Dance Performance." *Critical Studies/Critical Methodologies* 12 (1): 67–71. http://dx.doi.org/10.1177/1532708611430491

Bateson, G., and Margaret Mead. 1942. *Balinese Character: A Photographic Analysis*. New York: New York Academy of Sciences.

Benjamin, Walter. 2002. *The Arcades Project*, ed. Rolf Tiedemann, trans. Howard Eiland and Kevin McLaughlin. New York: Belknap Press.

Blackman, Lisa. 2009. "The Re-Making of Sexual Kinds: Queer Subjects and the Limits of Representation." *Journal of Lesbian Studies* 13 (2): 122–35. http://dx.doi.org/10.1080/10894160802695312

Blackman, Lisa. 2011. "Affect, Performance and Queer Subjectivity." *Cultural Studies* 25 (2): 183–99. http://dx.doi.org/10.1080/09502386.2011.535986

Buckland, Theresa, ed. 1999. *Dance in The Field: Theory, Methods and Issues in Dance Ethnography*. London: Palgrave Macmillan.

Classen, Constance. 1998. *Worlds of Sense: Exploring the Senses in History and across Cultures*. London: Routledge.

Classen, Constance. 2012. *The Deepest Sense: A Cultural History of Touch*. Champaign: University of Illinois Press.

Classen, Constance, David Howes, and Anthony Synnott, eds. 1994. *Aroma: The Cultural History of Smell*. London/New York: Routledge.

Conquergood, Dwight. 1991. "Rethinking Ethnography: Towards a Critical Cultural Politics." *Communication Monographs* 58 (2): 179–94. http://dx.doi.org/10.1080/03637759109376222

Coulthard, Glen. 2014. *Red Skin, White Masks: Rejecting the Colonial Politics of Recognition*. Minneapolis: University of Minnesota Press. http://dx.doi.org/10.5749/minnesota/9780816679645.001.0001

Csordas, Thomas. 1993. "Somatic Modes of Attention." *Cultural Anthropology* 8 (2): 135–56. http://dx.doi.org/10.1525/can.1993.8.2.02a00010

Csordas, Thomas. 2013. "Somatic Modes of Attention: Interview with Thomas Csordas." *Cultural Anthropology*. https://culanth.org/articles/301-somatic-modes-of-attention

Culhane, Dara. 2015. "Smile! It's Your NLI: Nine Scenes from a Sensory Ethnography." *Performance Matters* 1 (1–2): 76–100.

Davida, Dena, ed. 2011. *Fields in Motion: Ethnography in the Worlds of Dance*. Waterloo, ON: Wilfrid Laurier University Press.

Desjarlais, Robert, and C. Jason Throop. 2011. "Phenomenological Approaches in Anthropology." *Annual Review of Anthropology* 40 (1): 87–102. http://dx.doi.org/10.1146/annurev-anthro-092010-153345

Elliott, Denielle. 2014. "Truth, Shame, Complicity, and Flirtation: An Unconventional Ethnographic (Non)Fiction." *Anthropology and Humanism* 39 (2): 145–58. http://dx.doi.org/10.1111/anhu.12052

Feld, Steven. 1982. *Sound and Sentiment: Birds, Weeping, Poetics and Song in Kaluli Expression*. Philadelphia: University of Pennsylvania Press.

Feld, Steven. 1994. "From Ethnomusicology to Echo-Muse-Ecology: Reading R. Murray Schafer in the Papua New Guinea Rainforest." *The Soundscape Newsletter*, World Forum for Acoustic Ecology, 8 (June): 9–13. 10. http://wfae.net/library/articles/feld-ethnomusicology.pdf

Feld, Steven, and Donald Brenneis. 2004. "Doing Anthropology in Sound." *American Ethnologist* 31 (4): 461–74. http://dx.doi.org/10.1525/ae.2004.31.4.461

Fine, Sean. 2015. "Chief Justice Says Canada Attempted 'Cultural Genocide' on Aboriginals." *Globe and Mail*, 28 May. http://www.theglobeandmail.com/news/national/chief-justice-says-canada-attempted-cultural-genocide-on-aboriginals/article24688854

Flynn, Alex, and Jonas Tinius, eds. 2015. *Anthropology, Theatre and Development: The Transformative Potential of Performance.* London: Palgrave Macmillan. http://dx.doi.org/10.1057/9781137350602

Glass, Aaron. 2004. "The Thin Edge of the Wedge: Dancing around the Potlatch Ban, 1921–1951." In *Right to Dance: Dancing for Rights,* ed. Nancy M. Jackson, 51–82. Banff, AB: Banff Centre Press.

Gupta, A. and J. Ferguson, eds. 1997. *Culture, Power and Place: Explorations in Critical Anthropology.* Durham, NC: Duke University Press.

Harbers, Hans, Annemarie Mol, and Alice Stollmeyer. 2002. "Food Matters: Arguments for an Ethnography of Daily Care." *Theory, Culture & Society* 19 (5–6): 207–26. http://dx.doi.org/10.1177/026327602761899228

Herzfeld, Michael. 2008. "Senses." In *Ethnographic Fieldwork: An Anthropological Reader,* eds. Antonius C.G.M. Robben and Jeffrey A. Sluka, 431–42. Oxford: Blackwell.

Hockey, John, and Jacquelyn Allen-Collinson. 2009. "The Sensorium at Work: The Sensory Phenomenology of the Working Body." *Sociological Review* 57 (2): 217–39. http://dx.doi.org/10.1111/j.1467-954X.2009.01827.x

Howes, David, ed. 1991. *The Varieties of Sensory Experience: A Sourcebook in the Anthropology of the Senses.* Toronto: University of Toronto Press.

Howes, David, ed. 2004. *Empire of the Senses: The Sensual Culture Reader.* Oxford: Berg.

Howes, David. 2005. "Hyperesthesia, or, the Sensual Logic of Late Capitalism." In *Empire of the Senses: The Sensual Culture Reader,* ed. David Howes, 281–303. Oxford: Berg.

Howes, David, ed. 2009. *The Sixth Sense Reader.* Oxford: Berg.

Howes, David. 2010. "Response to Sarah Pink." *Social Anthropology* 18 (3): 333–36, 338–40. http://dx.doi.org/10.1111/j.1469-8676.2010.00119_2.x

Howes, David. 2011. "Reply to Tim Ingold." *Social Anthropology* 19 (3): 318–22, 328–31. http://dx.doi.org/10.1111/j.1469-8676.2011.00164.x

Howes, David. 2013. "The Expanding Field of Sensory Studies." *Sensory Studies.* http://www.sensorystudies.org/sensorial-investigations/the-expanding-field-of-sensory-studies

Howes, David, and Constance Classen. 2014. *Ways of Sensing: Understanding The Senses in Society.* London: Routledge.

Ingold, Tim. 2011a. *Being Alive: Essays on Movement, Knowledge and Description.* London: Routledge.

Ingold, Tim. 2011b. "Worlds of Sense and Sensing the World: A Response to David Howes." *Social Anthropology* 19 (3): 313–17. http://dx.doi.org/10.1111/j.1469-8676.2011.00163.x

Irving, Andrew. 2013. "Bridges: A New Sense of Scale." *Senses and Society* 8 (3): 290–313. http://dx.doi.org/10.2752/174589313X13712175020514

Katzman, Erika R. 2015. "Embodied Reflexivity: Knowledge and the Body in Professional Practice." In *The Body in Professional Practice, Learning and Education: Professional and Practice-Based Learning,* vol. 11, eds. Bill Green and Nick Hopwood, 157–72. Cham, Switzerland: Springer International. http://dx.doi.org/10.1007/978-3-319-00140-1_10

Madison, D. Soyini. 2011. "It's Time to Write: Writing as Performance." *Critical Ethnography: Method, Ethics, and Performance*, 209–32. London: Sage.

Magnat, Virginie. 2011. "Conducting Embodied Research at the Intersection of Performance Studies, Experimental Ethnography, and Indigenous Methodologies." *Anthropologica* 53 (2): 213–27.

Manalansan, Martin F. 2006. "Immigrant Lives and the Politics of Olfaction in the Global City." In *The Smell Culture Reader*, ed. Jim Drobnick, 41–52. Oxford: Berg.

Mascia-Lees, Frances, ed. 2011. *A Companion to the Anthropology of the Body and Embodiment*. New York: Wiley-Blackwell.

Mead, Margaret. [1974] 2003. "Visual Anthropology in a Discipline of Words." In *Principles of Visual Anthropology*, 3rd ed., ed. Paul Hockings, 4. Berlin: Mouton de Gruyter.

Million, Dian. 2013. *Therapeutic Nations: Healing in an Age of Indigenous Human Rights*. Tucson: University of Arizona Press.

Moretti, Cristina. 2015. *Milanese Encounters: Public Space and Vision in Contemporary Urban Italy*. Toronto: University of Toronto Press.

Pink, Sarah. 2008. "An Urban Tour: The Sensory Sociality of Ethnographic Place-Making." *Ethnography* 9 (2): 175–96. http://dx.doi.org/10.1177/1466138108089467

Pink, Sarah. 2010. "Response to David Howes." *Social Anthropology* 18 (3): 336–38. http://dx.doi.org/10.1111/j.1469-8676.2010.00119_3.x

Pink, Sarah. 2015. *Doing Sensory Ethnography*. London: Palgrave.

Porcello, Thomas, Louise Meintjes, Ana Maria Ochoa, and David W. Samuels. 2010. "The Reorganization of the Sensory World." *Annual Review of Anthropology* 39 (1): 51–66. http://dx.doi.org/10.1146/annurev.anthro.012809.105042

Robben, Antonius C.G.M. 2008. "Introduction: Sensorial Fieldwork." In *Ethnographic Fieldwork: An Anthropological Reader*, eds. Antonius C.G.M. Robben and Jeffrey A. Sluka, 385–88. Oxford: Blackwell.

Robertson, Leslie A., and Kwaguł Gixsam Clan. 2012. *Standing up with Ga'axstal'las: Jane Constance Cook and the Politics of Memory, Church and Custom*. Vancouver: University of British Columbia Press.

Rooke, Alison. 2009. "Queer in the Field: On Emotion, Temporality and Performativity in Ethnography." *Journal of Lesbian Studies* 13 (2): 149–60. http://dx.doi.org/10.1080/10894160802695338

Rosaldo, Renato. 2013. *The Day of Shelly's Death: The Poetry and Ethnography of Grief*. Durham, NC: Duke University Press. http://dx.doi.org/10.1215/9780822376736

Roth-Gordon, Jennifer. 2013. "Racial Malleability and the Sensory Regime of Politically Conscious Brazilian Hip Hop." *Journal of Latin American and Caribbean Anthropology* 18 (2): 294–313. http://dx.doi.org/10.1111/jlca.12021

Rouch, Jean, dir. 1955. *Les Maîtres Fous*. Ghana.

Rouch, Jean, and Edgar Morin, dirs. 1960. *Chronicle d'un été*. Paris.

Rouch, Jean, dir. 1970. *Petit à Petit*. Niger and France.

Sensory Ethnography Lab. n.d. Harvard University. Accessed 4 July 2015. https://sel.fas.harvard.edu

Simpson, Audra. 2014. *Mohawk Interruptus: Political Life across the Border of Settler States*. Durham, NC: Duke University Press. http://dx.doi.org/10.1215/9780822376781

Simpson, Audra, and Andrea Smith, eds. 2014. *Theorizing Native Studies*. Durham, NC: Duke University Press. http://dx.doi.org/10.1215/9780822376613

Stewart, Kathleen. 2007. *Ordinary Affects*. Durham, NC: Duke University Press. http://dx.doi.org/10.1215/9780822390404

Stoller, Paul. 1989. *The Taste of Ethnographic Things: The Senses in Anthropology*. Philadelphia: University of Pennsylvania Press.

Stoller, Paul. 1992. *The Cinematic Griot: The Ethnography of Jean Rouch*. Chicago: University of Chicago Press.

Stoller, Paul. 1997. *Sensuous Scholarship*. Philadelphia: University of Pennsylvania Press.

Stoller, Paul. 1999. *Jaguar: A Story of Africans in America*. Chicago: University of Chicago Press.

Stoller, Paul. 2002. *Money Has No Smell: The Africanization of New York City*. Chicago: University of Chicago Press. http://dx.doi.org/10.7208/chicago/9780226775265.001.0001

Wulff, Helena. 2007. *Dancing at the Crossroads: Memory and Mobility in Ireland*. New York: Berghahn Books.

Notes

1 Stoller writes creative non-fiction, fiction, and memoir, as well as columns in public media and articles in professional journals and academic publications.

2 Irving's article is available as text-and-image essay, and online in audio and audio-visual formats.

CHAPTER 4

RECORDING AND EDITING

Alexandrine Boudreault-Fournier

Introduction

Digital devices such as cell phones and GoPro cameras are now part of how we experience places, events and, more generally, our everyday normal life. People capture moments with their smartphones and share them almost instantaneously with networks of online friends and followers. Filters on Instagram allow aficionado photographers to play with the grain and colors of a digital picture, thereby altering its temporality and meaning. As these devices, programs, and applications become part of our normal life, some people are raising concerns about how overusing smartphones and similar devices might negatively transform our perceptions of the world and the quality of our social relationships. These critics voice concerns over the exaggerated mediation of those devices, a mediation that, in their view, might be leading to a mediocre and less sensual appreciation of our environment and our social relationships.

IMAGE 4.1: Listening at the Royal BC Museum.

Credit: Chris O'Connor, 2014.

This chapter takes a different approach than such critics by arguing against the idea that recording devices promote a disorienting effect on our senses (see also Sterne 2003). Rather, it explores the ways in which we can use recording devices, such as cameras, sound recorders, and smartphones, to creatively and imaginatively relate with the various environments in which we conduct research. I am encouraging not an oversaturation of audiovisual recording, but rather a conscious focus on the process of how we record, how we select certain images and sounds, and how we discard others through the processes of recording and, later, through editing. Editing can be defined as the process through which audiovisual clips are juxtaposed to produce a storyline (Marcus 1990, 2013). It is a process that is at the heart of the filmic narrative because it establishes associations between clips that might not otherwise have any relationship to one another. In this chapter, I use the terms "montage" and "editing" interchangeably to refer to the "joining together of different elements in a variety of combinations, repetitions, and overlaps" (Willerslev and Suhr 2013, 1).[1] In contrast to the term "editing," "montage" has been traditionally associated with cinematographic and aesthetic genres such as those of Soviet, French, and American film. Yet, because I am interested in the process of cutting, pasting, and playing with visual and sound clips—mainly in digital formats—to create a narrative, I am less interested in defining these genres (although I briefly touch on this below) than in exploring the ways in which the montage process connects with imagination.

While the concept of montage is associated with different artistic disciplines, this chapter focuses more specifically on audiovisual media, and therefore it delves into cinema, visual anthropology, sound, and sensory studies, areas that are associated with abundant literary traditions. Obviously, this chapter cannot cover them all. However, it is worth mentioning that anthropologists have for a long time used film and sound recording devices to collect data. Recording endangered cultural practices, argues Margaret Mead ([1974] 2003), allows anthropologists to preserve the cultures under study in providing concrete material for analysis. The Alan Lomax sound archive constituting more than 17,000 recordings of songs, interviews, and other sonic traces collected from the 1940s into the 1990s is an example of this type of approach. Despite the acknowledgment that film and sound recording devices are essential to ethnographic fieldwork, the use of film and sound recording devices remained a challenge until recently for most anthropologists not used to the technology. Also, remember that in comparison to video, film necessitated heavy and expensive equipment. The emergence of digital technologies democratized the access to recording devices and to editing software. This had a huge impact in anthropology as the production of audiovisual material became more accessible.

The history of visual anthropology is rich and complex (see for instance Banks and Morphy 1997; Pink 2001; Hockings 2003; Ruby 2000; Marcus and Ruby 2011) and although there has been an extensive literature on the analysis of films and photography in anthropology, few address the concrete technicalities of recording and editing audiovisual texts (Barbash and Taylor 1997 being one exception). The production of audiovisual texts in anthropology now encompasses the traditional approach to ethnographic filmmaking. Some produce multimedia installation; others are interested in the potentials of performance, artistic collaboration, and experimentation (for instance, Schneider and Wright 2013b; Schneider and Pasqualino 2014; see more below). The Sensory Ethnography Lab at Harvard University, directed by Lucien Castaing-Taylor, and the Centre for Sensory Studies at Concordia University, directed by David Howes, encourage creative works and investigations—through the use of recording and editing techniques, among others—that explore aesthetics and the senses from an anthropological perspective.

Inspired by these novel approaches that combine creativity and the senses, this chapter focuses on one main argument, namely that sound and image recording and editing processes act not as barriers to perceptions and interpretations, but, on the contrary, as catalysts that encourage researchers and students to reflect upon where they stand, with whom, and how. In other words, I establish a strong relationship between the recording and editing of visual and sound clips on the one hand, and the concept of imagination on the other.

Technologies and techniques to capture sensorial experiences such as touch, smell, and taste do exist. For instance, the frottis technique in fine arts allows for a visual representation of textures that evokes different feelings of touch. Perfumery could be approached as a technology that archives smells and aromas. Yet, to this day, no technology allows for the recording and editing of these sensorial experiences, at least not in the way digital audiovisual recording devices do. Digital recording devices allow for easy capturing, archiving, retrieval, and consumption of sonic and visual clips. Yet, it would be misleading to argue that audiovisual clips relate only to the senses of vision and hearing. When we watch audiovisual media, our imagination is not bound to visuals and sounds; these media connect us with other realms of experiencing and sensing. In this sense, films stimulate our imagination! The film *Chocolat* (2000) directed by Lasse Holström is an excellent example of how films can open up our imagination to other worlds of senses and places. When actress Juliette Binoche carefully prepares the chocolate, one cannot but imagine the smell and the taste of this precious delicacy (in fact, viewers should be warned that they might suffer from a chocolate rush while watching the film!). Sarah Pink argues that visual recordings can become "routes to multisensory knowing" (Pink 2009, 99). The senses are interconnected, and we need to understand them in practice and through the act of making (Ingold 2000, 2013), which could refer to many things such as walking (see Cristina Moretti's chapter, "Walking," in this volume) and writing (see Denielle Elliott's chapter, "Writing," in this volume), and—more relevant to this chapter—through recording and editing audiovisual media.

This chapter takes as a starting point that "theory is now in the way of making, rather than outside it" (Schneider and Wright 2013a, 1) and that it is through the process of doing and creating that anthropologists should conduct fieldwork. Research is a creative process (Sullivan 2010) and anthropologists must be understood as creative agents and producer-researchers in addition to participant-observers (Boudreault-Fournier 2012, 2016). Imagination serves this purpose because it opens doors to creativity and experimentation, and by consequence, toward novel ways of exploring, making, and sensing. Anthropologists engage with images and sounds with their cameras and their sound recorders, and they connect with these dimensions in the process of recording and editing. Students who are used to interacting with digital media and tools can also learn from in-depth engagement in creating audiovisual media. Yet, the making and creating of audiovisual media within an ethnographic context and as part of an active interaction with the social and material environment needs to be explored further, as it has received little attention in anthropology up to now.

"Cinematic Imagination"

Anthropology has had no lack of interest in the visual; its problem has always been what to do with it.

—David MacDougall (2006, 213)

David MacDougall's "cinematic imagination" (MacDougall 2006, 2009), which he borrows from the work of George Marcus (1990), is a rich concept by which to think about both recording and editing on the one hand, and imagination on the other. This concept, which connects the disciplines of theater, cinema, literature, film studies, and visual anthropology, encourages us to think in terms of doing and learning in the process of creating video and/or sound media. To provide some brief background on the concept of "cinematic imagination," how MacDougall applies it, and how it relates to practices of recording and editing, let us first address George Marcus's understanding of the concept.

When George Marcus discusses the term "cinematic imagination," he refers to the ways in which the technique of montage in cinema is increasingly becoming a source of inspiration for writing ethnographies. George Marcus was among the anthropologists in the 1980s who raised a series of criticisms of the discipline of anthropology (see Clifford and Marcus 1986). These critics mainly targeted the ways in which anthropologists traditionally conducted fieldwork and wrote ethnographies. We could briefly summarize some of this criticism in three points:

1. Polyphony, which refers to the importance of including various voices in ethnographic writing—so that the anthropologist's voice is not the only one to be considered;
2. Fragmentation, which encourages the anthropologist to think in terms of incompleteness, nonlinearity, and partial truth; and
3. Reflexivity, which raises the issue of the anthropologist's position, its subjectivity, and, by consequence, the challenges that must be addressed to achieve objectivity.

The critics also targeted issues of representation—who can represent whom?—the temporality of ethnographic accounts, which tended to position the other as not living in the same timeframe as the researcher (also see Fabian 1983), and the issue of a settled community of research. These marked a shift in the "anthropological imagination" where the world is perceived as being no longer complete and coherent, but rather fragmented and ambiguous (MacDougall 2006, 244).

George Marcus (1990) observes that anthropologists began to adapt their writing practices to these criticisms as well as to novel situations they could no longer ignore, such as the deterritorialized nature of culture and the simultaneous existence of multiple worlds in a context of globalization. He characterizes this emergent style of writing as "modern" and as addressing these criticisms, in contrast to a more realist approach to ethnography, which is no longer suitable for the world in which we live.

Marcus (1990) further suggests that anthropologists should continue to look to cinema for inspiration, and more specifically to the technique of montage, which can serve different purposes. Montage can create a fluid narrative so that a series of sequences look natural and distortion free. In contrast, it can also produce a sense of fragmentation and disturbance to amplify the idea that a cinematic narrative is an artificial discourse and that it should not be taken for granted by the spectator. The former example refers to a fluid style of montage known as "continuity editing" and often associated with American cinema. The latter example corresponds to a more disruptive style, sometimes labeled "intellectual cinema" and traditionally associated with Soviet cinema, and more particularly with the works of the famous early Soviet filmmakers Eisenstein and Dziga Vertov (MacDougall 2006). Ethnographic filmmaking has conventionally followed an observational style, which favored techniques of montage that would maximally respect ordinary lived time and space, or what has often been referred to as the "fly on the wall" approach to filmmaking. These different approaches to montage have an impact on how a film's narrative is constructed and, by consequence, how it is interpreted by spectators.

The idea developed by Marcus is that writing can reflect cinematographic effects, and more specifically, it can echo the techniques associated with montage. For instance, one montage technique is known as "parallel" or "cross-cutting," which refers to the subsequent alternation between two sequences. The dialogue between the juxtaposed sequences generates a sense of simultaneity: different events happen at the same time but in two localities. A similar meaning can be conveyed in ethnographic writing by juxtaposing two vignettes that develop two different stories. In using this technique, an anthropologist amplifies the idea of simultaneity between two different localities (modern writing) rather than suggesting a sense of geographical and temporal distance from the ethnographer (more linear and realist style of writing). In *Jackie Brown* (1997) and *Kill Bill* (2003/2004), the American film director Quentin Tarantino uses the juxtaposition of images in one frame to suggest that two scenes are happening at the same time but not at the same place.

MacDougall is inspired by Marcus's approach, yet he uses the term "cinematic imagination" in a different way. According to MacDougall (2006), "cinematic imagination" came before the invention of cinema. It consists of ways of thinking, such as visual ontologies, that paved the way for the invention of cinema as a technology and for the emergence of the cinematographic genre as we experience it today. One of the key characteristics of "cinematic imagination" is "a desire to create an interpretive space for the reader or spectator" (245). It is a mode of writing or a cinematographic experience that allows the reader/viewer to relate to the experience of the author/filmmaker through a series of descriptions/sequences. "Structuring a work in this way," argues MacDougall, "involves a multipositional perspective that acknowledges the fragmentary nature of experience and, by extension, the constructed nature of human knowledge" (245–46). This way of writing and of editing films situates the reader/viewer not outside of a text but at its center, MacDougall argues. It further brings into play the viewer's ability to share someone else's consciousness while watching a film; it is about being involved imaginatively with a film. The scene of a woman taking a shower in Alfred Hitchcock's film *Psycho* is frightening because we project ourselves to the center of the action as if we could feel the fear personally, imagining ourselves standing under the hot water and at the mercy of an assassin whose presence is sensed behind the curtain.

Both Marcus and MacDougall argue that the advent of montage techniques in cinema, and the shift in the "anthropological imagination" that led to the crisis of representation in the 1980s, happened almost independently of each other. According to MacDougall, only after World War II did cinema and anthropology begin to converge and did anthropologists open up to experimenting with the visual (MacDougall 2006, 2009). As a consequence, new forms of "cinematographic writing styles" in anthropology were not necessarily exploited in ethnographic films until a later stage. This situation brings us back to the epigraph by MacDougall mentioned above: it indeed took a long time for anthropologists to know what to do with the visual (not to mention sound, an interest that has only been growing in anthropology over the last few years). MacDougall (2006) cites two exceptions to this observation: the ethnographer-filmmakers Jean Rouch and John Marshall:

> Rouch and Marshall believed that visual anthropology could and should do more than simply record what was in front of the camera. They were after the invisible content of the scenes they filmed, both in terms of the sense of space they conveyed and the experience of individuals. They respected the film-viewer's ability to grasp the fact that life continues even when the camera is not actually showing it. (62)

Their grand achievement, MacDougall (2006) explains, was to provide enough clues for the viewer to *re-imagine* the world in which the film's subjects lived, despite all of the invisible elements that were not included because they remained outside of the camera angle. The re-imagination process, which takes place at the time of the film's reception, refers to the spectator's own appropriation, interpretation, and imagining of the place, time, and context in which the film was shot and where it takes place in the film narrative. This re-imagination might also include what is not shown in the film, that is, what is not visible but only suggested. This process of re-imagination allows the viewer to appreciate a film and to understand it in all its complexity.

Despite the late start of ethnographic films in developing, adapting, and experimenting with innovative forms of montage, some visual anthropologists did propose creative editing practices to push the boundaries of what was considered an "ethnographic film." Jay Ruby (2000, 6) defines ethnographic films as being "confined to those works in which the maker had formal training in ethnography, [that are] intended to produce an ethnography, [that] employed ethnographic field practices, and [that] sought validation among those competent to judge the work as an ethnography." I adopt a more inclusive definition of ethnographic film. I believe that any film adopting an ethically conscious approach that is based on fieldwork (in a very broad sense) could be considered as ethnographic. Ethnographic films can be experimental, and they should encourage us to reflect on what are the boundaries of the discipline.

Innovative montage practices propose novel ways of using films to engage with feelings, emotions, memories, and sensitive topics such as death. *Forest of Bliss* (1986) by Robert Gardner is one striking example. Considered one of his most complex works from an editorial perspective, *Forest of Bliss* has received both positive appraisals and severe criticism (Henley 2007a). On the one hand, the film was considered an incredible source of inspiration for generations of visual anthropologists and students alike, but on the other, the film was denied any anthropological value whatsoever. One of the main criticisms of *Forest of Bliss*, which is about death in Varanasi, India, is its total absence of subtitles or helpful linguistic references, leaving spectators who do not speak Hindi to their own devices. At the same time that this absence significantly impacts viewers' understanding of the film, it also pushes them to pay particular attention to the symbolic and metaphorical nature of the images and sounds that were carefully recorded and selected for the film. Anthropologist and filmmaker Paul Henley (2007a) provides a good overview of some of the visual and sonic montage techniques that Gardner used to re-create the atmosphere that characterizes the city of Varanasi, situated on the banks of the Ganges, as well as the city's death-related activities. Only little by little, and often metaphorically, does the film reveal the elements and activities related to death. Chopped wood, for example, appears in different scenes, but only at a later stage does the spectator understand that the wood is used for pyres. In terms of montage, Henley gives the example of the use of juxtaposed clips, a serial form of montage, to suggest how death is viewed as part of life for all creatures, including humans. At one point in the film, a series of clips show dead animals being dragged down the *ghat* (the wide steps leading down to the river) and disposed of in the waters of the Ganges. These sequences are followed by images of an old blind man who is also seen going down the *ghat*. The meaning conveyed by this serial montage, argues Henley, is that "we too will one day die and, actually or metaphorically, will be taken down the steps of a ghat and disposed of in a river somewhere" (2007a, 45; Henley also refers to the discussion of this scene by Gardner and Östör 2001). Henley adds that the use of a series of similar images, relating parallel stories and juxtaposed one after the other, generates a form of metaphorical meaning.

The film *Lumina Amintirri* (*In the Light of Memory*, 2010), directed by Alyssa Grossman, is another example of mastering video montage to convey rather than depict meaning.[2] The film is about memory in post-communist Bucharest, Romania. To make a film on memory, an invisible element which is difficult to convey visually, Grossman decided to use a technique called "in-camera montage," which in her case consists of moving along horizontally while recording uninterrupted shots, what she describes as the bicycle "traveling" sequences (Grossman 2013), in which the viewer observes people sitting and relaxing on the park's old wooden benches. To shoot these scenes, Grossman strapped her camera to her bicycle saddle and filmed people sitting on the park's line of green benches throughout a long uninterrupted scene during which she made a full circle around the park. When subjected to Grossman's camera, many people look at her as if she is invading a private moment. Some seem to wonder what she is doing, while others don't even notice her. The traveling shots are extremely powerful. As spectators and outsiders, we feel a desire to learn more about these people; we are made to imagine their presence in relation to a past and a future of which we know little except what we garner from the physical presence of embodied memories. The complexity and multiplicity of individual and collective memory is beautifully orchestrated in the film by a fluid montage. Superimposed voices of interviewees—whom the viewer never gets to see—share memories over beautiful but mundane shots of the park. Our attention constantly shifts between images lived in present time and voices sending us back to stories of the past. About her choice of montage techniques, Grossman writes, "By experimenting with various techniques of montage, I sought to re-create an experience for my spectators that would be analogous to remembrance work. I wanted my film to critically examine memory by evoking how it operates and feels, rather than by explaining or depicting memories themselves" (Grossman 2013, 201). As a consequence, in *Lumina Amintirri*, the park becomes a space of imagination and memorialization.

It might appear to some readers that we have been focusing on montage primarily as a process of visual assemblage. Yet, I always tell my students that cinema is as much about sound as it is about the visual dimension. We all agree that it is irritating and even a waste of time to watch a film without sound. Sound is most often taken for granted and is not perceived by the spectator as meaningful in constructing the cinematic narrative. But this is part of the illusion and what gives sound all its power! Michel Chion (1994, 2003), a specialist of sound in cinema, argues that it is because sound is so much taken for granted that it becomes such a powerful dimension in filmmaking. Sound can be exploited to alter the moods of spectators without them noticing it. Chion (1994) calls the power of sound over images "added value." The term refers to the illusion that sound is unnecessary to cinema. To go back to the shower scene of *Psycho*, a stunning effect will be produced if one watches the scene first without music, then with the visual scene (without ambient sound) set to classical music, and finally the visual scene set to the song "Happy" by Pharrell Williams. The mood of the scene shifts from horror to nostalgia and finally humor. This simple exercise is enough to convince any skeptic about the power of sound in cinema.

Indeed, filmmakers know about sound's potential and play with it as much as they desire to transform spectators' perceptions. Significantly, in the domain of visual anthropology, there has been an argument to limit the use of sounds that are not natural to a scene. Jean Rouch claimed that "sound is the opium of cinema" (in Henley 2007b, 55) to criticize the potential power of sound to alter the meaning of a scene or a film. The argument made by Rouch is that sounds that are not part of a recorded scene can create false impressions and should not be used to generate "artificial meanings" in ethnographic films. In many ways, this echoes the suspicion surrounding the concept of montage more generally in anthropology, which is regarded as a polluting process that would disrupt the relationship between scholarly representation and the social world (Willerslev and Suhr 2013, 1).

Although visual anthropologists recognize the potential of sound to alter a filmic narrative, not all agree with the "purist" sonic approach put forward by Jean Rouch. Henley (2007b), for instance, argues that ethnographers should use sounds more creatively and effectively in ethnographic filmmaking. Sounds that are neither verbal nor musical, argues Henley, can add a rich experiential dimension to communication. Similar to providing a thick description *à la* Clifford Geertz, sound can become key to deepening the representation of a place or an event in a film. In other words, a creative use of sound through montage techniques has the potential to thicken the implicit ethnographic description. Henley suggests that filmmakers should record sounds where video scenes are captured—independently from filming—to create a bank of sounds that can later be added to the original soundtrack to thicken the visual ethnographic description. He further argues that such a use of sound can enhance the spectator's understanding of the subject presented in the film as well as enhance the modes by which the filmmaker proposes an interpretation of the film's subject matter (Henley 2007b, 56). I certainly believe in the creative potential of sound in audiovisual media production, but I would not eliminate the use of extrasonic clips such as music and language in ethnographic filmmaking. Sound, understood in all of its dimensions, can add to the "cinematic imagination" by contributing what we could refer to as "sonic imagination."

Jonathan Sterne (2012) uses the term "sonic imaginations" to refer to how sound is imagined culturally and historically. He explains that "sound students" should explore sonic imaginations from a critical perspective. As he writes, sonic imaginations "are necessarily plural, recursive, reflexive, driven to represent, refigure and redescribe" (2012, 5). Both Sterne's and MacDougall's uses of imagination include a historically embedded approach to the sonic and the visual respectively, in considering the emergence and development of technologies that impact how we sense, perceive, and interpret our world. As such, we should also use "cinematic imaginations" in the plural to reflect the diversity of perceptions and interpretations that can emerge from audiovisual media.

The audio documentary, a type of medium that does not rely on visual media, also calls for the concept of imagination in a similar way to how it is developed by MacDougall. The process of editing audio documentaries involves techniques of recording, capturing, cutting, and superimposing on the timeline that are similar to those used in film editing. For example, the sound documentary *Ghetto Life 101* (1993) about everyday life in Chicago's South Side was created by two young boys, Lealan Jones, 13 years old, and Lloyd Newman, 14 years old, in collaboration with radio producer David Isay.[3] In listening to this world-acclaimed sound documentary, one notices all the techniques that were used during recording and editing to capture both the vivid and rough life of these two young boys. Music, walking steps, barking dogs, laughter, voice-overs, and direct voice recordings are all examples of different sources of sounds that are used to allow the listener to imagine the scenes, the characters, and the atmospheres associated with the South Side ghetto.

If we come back to the concept of "cinematic imagination" as developed by MacDougall, it is obvious how films, sound media, and more specifically techniques of montage generate worlds in which spectators and listeners can *re-imagine* the places, events, atmospheres, and activities (among other things) that are represented in a film or a sound clip. Spectators might connect with the media in a very personal and intimate manner, provoking emotions and sensorial impressions. The examples developed above demonstrate how filmmakers and media producers in general carefully and consciously record and edit images and sounds to convey certain meanings or at least to generate metaphorical and symbolic references. Therefore, the "cinematic imagination" corresponds to ways of sensing and imagining visually and cinematically, as well as to ways of re-imagining through the viewing and listening of an audiovisual medium. To sum up, the "cinematic imagination" is then an approach that plays out when a filmmaker records images and sounds and edits a film; it also applies to when people watch or listen to audiovisual or sonic media.

Recording

Recording involves a careful attention to where one stands. It is about sensing the visual and sonic details that one wishes to collect. In the documentary film *Soundtracker* (2010), Gordon Hempton, presented as a sound hunter, travels all over the United States to record sounds he believes are valuable from a sonic and environmental perspective. Gordon Hempton is extremely conscious of the sonic world that surrounds him, and he carefully chooses the places where he records sounds. The film shows Hempton being frustrated at the sound of an electric generator in a deserted field. He cries at the sound of a plane flying over a national park reserve. For him, this sound pollution, or noise, does not allow him to appreciate (and record) the site in all of its natural complexity and beauty. Of course, this is an extreme example of a "way of sensing" and, obviously, Hempton is a convinced romantic environmentalist. Yet, we all, at different levels, shift our attention to what surrounds us at the time of recording a landscape, a song, or even a birthday party. We may attempt to alter what we believe contaminates what we wish to capture, in turning off a radio or turning on the light, to record as faithfully as possible, thanks to the recording device, what we wish to preserve and how we want it to be preserved. Recording awakens our senses and pushes us to become more aware of our surroundings.

Similarly, Sarah Pink (2009) discusses how anthropologists, when using a recording device, such as a camera, engage with social and material environments through a mode of sensorial participation. This engagement with place, according to Pink, occurs at three levels. The first level refers to anthropologists' presence in a place through their body and their senses, as well as through their camera. Anthropologists using a camera and a sound recorder engage with the environment in specific ways. They are carefully walking with the senses tuned in. The camera is never detached from the anthropologist-with-a-video-camera; it moves along with researchers as they explore various places and it becomes somewhat part of their identity. As a consequence, Pink argues, ethnographers cannot remove themselves from the audiovisual recording. The presence of ethnographers in recordings is what David MacDougall (2006) calls "corporeal images."

The "corporeal sounds" (to apply MacDougall's term to the sonic dimension) are also present in a sound clip. A microphone captures all surrounding sounds, and it is tiresome to target only one sound without "contaminating" the recording with other ambient sounds. It is also difficult to eliminate one's presence from a sound recording, even with the use of a unidirectional microphone. Therefore, recording allows the anthropologist to develop an acute sensorial approach. It further connects the anthropologist to a place, in leaving sonic and visual traces on the raw footage, which can only be altered (but not totally erased) subsequently in the editing suite.

The specific criteria and parameters established by the filmmaker refer to the second level of engagement with a place mentioned by Sarah Pink. The filmmaker makes many decisions that impact what is being recorded (and what is not) and how. For instance, how is the camera positioned, what is the camera recording, and what angles are selected? Those decisions have a direct impact on a film's aesthetics, meaning, and narrative. These choices are based on the intentions of the filmmaker to represent a place in a specific way. Filming is about imagining ways of representing a social and material environment. In all these ways, the nature of the clip itself contributes to create another interpretation of a place based on the perception of the filmmaker.

The third level of engagement with a place through the use of a camera by an anthropologist, according to Pink, corresponds to the moment when an audience (which includes the ethnographer) watches and listens to the recordings and uses "their imaginations to create personal/cultural understandings of the representation" (Pink 2009, 101). This refers to the process of re-imagination on the part of the audience, that is, a re-imagination of the interpretation made by the filmmaker, based on his or her own imagining of a place.

Although Pink addresses visual recording devices (video) more specifically, a similar argument could be applied to sound recording. Hildegard Westerkamp (2002), a Canadian composer and sound artist, writes that a fundamental feature of sound composition is intensive listening, both directly with the ears and via the microphone, a process that engages both creator and listener directly in their environment. When recording sound, one needs to pay attention to what can be heard and to what is perceived as an annoyance (often referred to as noise). As a result, creators must develop greater awareness of their ambient soundscapes.

"Soundscape," a term associated with the works of R. Murray Schafer ([1977] 1994), Barry Truax (2001), and the members of the World Soundscape Project at Simon Fraser University on the West Coast of Canada, refers to any acoustic field of study, to the events heard, and to our sonic environment (Schafer [1977] 1994). The term also refers to the act of composing original sonic arrangements based on sonic recordings of a place (Schafer [1977] 1994). As Eylul Iscen (2014) explains, soundscape composition or soundscape editing is "a context-based composition where knowledge of specific contexts shapes the composer's work and invokes the listener's knowledge of those contexts . . . at the intersections of the listener's associations, memories and imaginations related to that place" (127).

Editing

The recording and subsequent editing of sound into a sound clip—the equivalent of film editing but with sound—requires imagination on the part of the composer attempting to evoke a specific place or situation. Montage (or editing) according to Marcus (2013, 305) involves a process that is similar to ethnographic fieldwork; it is about "being immersed in observations-being-made-into-representations." Sound recordings and edited sound clips are more abstract representations of the "real" compared to audiovisual media, yet they have greater potential to stimulate the listeners' memory, sensory experience, imagination, and mental worlds (Marcus 2013). In other words, sound clips require more active participation of our imagination and our memories. When listening carefully to a recorded soundscape, it is recommended to close one's eyes to limit visual disturbances and better concentrate on the sounds themselves. As a result, a listener can better imagine the scenes, situations, and places in relation with the recording.

It is clear that technology plays a significant role in the perception of an acoustic environment, and consequently it has an impact on the process of composing a soundscape (Truax 2012). Both as a process and as a finished product, soundscape composition or sound editing can tie the experience of sound back to the environment and foster increased spatial awareness (Labelle 2011). As previously mentioned, engaging with and recording the sounds of a place is part of constructing the representation of that place; it is about connecting and engaging with an environment through our imagination. Here again, the same argument can be applied to audiovisual media.

Yet, one engages with an environment not only through the audiovisual recordings of a place, but also through the conscious transformation of clips into a meaningful form of representation, be it a film, a clip, or a sound composition. Consequently, the process of editing sounds and images into original compositions and clips could be considered as corresponding to the practice of ethnography, the "anthropological imagination" in the words of MacDougall. Editing forces the researcher to select the clips that are considered as meaningful to represent a specific situation or a place. Editing can be understood as selecting, cutting, and organizing clips to create a space or a scene from raw video and sound footage that can reproduce, in some ways, the sensorial impressions felt at the time of the collection (see Drever 2002 on soundscape). Editing a soundscape and a video clip becomes a long and challenging process through which the ethnographer is making sense of raw recorded footage by producing a meaningful representation of a specific place or a situation. But this representation does not need to be "realistic"; it can take multiple forms and aesthetics. The entire editing process takes place through an imaginative construction of place.[4] In this sense, I argue that we can add a fourth level to the model proposed by Sarah Pink, as stated earlier. This fourth level would correspond to how we connect with a place, and how we imagine it, through the process of editing raw video and sound footage into a clip.

During a research project about back alleys in Vancouver, Nick Wees and I recorded sound and video clips to provide a sensorial engagement with back alleys, first through the process of capturing video and sound footage, and second through editing a series of clips (see Image 4.2). The clip "Soundscape and Videoscape—Back Alley Vancouver"[5] shows everyday uses of back alleys. Notice the small details and the sound of the electric infrastructure. The "Acoustic of a Saxophone Player in Vancouver's Back Alley"[6] video clip shows a saxophone player performing in a Vancouver downtown back alley. We created this clip to experiment with sensorial perceptions associated with this urban liminal space (Boudreault-Fournier and Wees, forthcoming).

In a totally different context, I produced, in collaboration with two Brazilian visual anthropologists, a "cinematic imagination" of a mundane scene from the

IMAGE 4.2: Recording in Vancouver's back alley.

Credit: Alexandrine Boudreault-Fournier, 2013.

football World Cup in Brazil during the summer of 2014.[7] The clip shows how a group of Brazilians, living in the periphery of the megacity São Paulo, watch and interact with each other during a football game involving their favorite team. Notice the colors, the sounds, the tension, and the interaction between the participants. Watching these clips stimulates a connection with these places, and this shows the power of the "cinematic imagination."

Student Exercises

In light of the concept of "cinematic imagination" discussed above, I would like to suggest two exercises that aim at refining our appreciation of the social and material environments that surround us, as well as encouraging us to think in terms of interpreting this environment using recording devices and our imagination. The two exercises address the following main question: How can we create a simple but meaningful visual or sonic representation of a place or a process?

1. Producing a Sequence

For the first exercise you will need a photo camera, a smartphone, or any other device that allows you to take pictures. The main idea of the exercise is to create a series of photos that will represent a process, a simple story, or a narrative. You may use no more than five photos for your final sequence.

For instance, if you are on a university campus and it is lunchtime, you might go to the cafeteria and take pictures of someone ordering and paying for lunch. Once this is done, select a maximum of five photos and organize them into a PowerPoint presentation project. Try to do this exercise within a time-frame of approximately 10–15 minutes. Once your PowerPoint presentation is ready, show your sequence to your friends. The sequence of the pictures should tell a story based on your interpretation of a process or a place. Are your friends interpreting the same thing as you wanted to convey? If not, why? How does your interpretation differ compared to those of your friends? How could your sequence have been more effective?

Variation: A similar exercise can be conducted with a video camera. Take a video camera and try to capture a process in planning a series of shots to create a storyline. For instance, you might decide to film your roommate preparing dinner. Start from the beginning of the process. Try to film key aspects and gestures that characterize the process using close, medium, and long shots. Use the pause key to stop filming; then choose what will be the next scene and press the record key again to resume recording. Repeat this process until you are happy with the sequence you recorded. Let the images speak for themselves and try not to impose a description of the process while you are recording. You may use basic editing software like iMovie to order the clips one after the other into a linear montage. Once the process is filmed and the clips ordered, watch your film and try to identify if the process is unfolding in a comprehensive way. Show it to your friends and discuss what they think the story/process is. Does it differ from your intention?

2. Soundwalk

In his book The *Soundscape: Our Sonic Environment and the Tuning of the World* ([1977] 1994), R. Murray Schafer provides a series of exercises to clear our ears and develop our ability of better listening to the surrounding envi-ronment. Exercises to clear our ears include stop making sounds for a while, declare a moratorium on speech for a full day, and meditate by focusing on one specific sound. "Soundwalk" is another method proposed by Schafer. He explains that a soundwalk is more than just taking a walk and listening to the sounds on the way. It is "an exploration of the soundscape in a given area using a score as a guide" ([1977] 1994, 213). The score is like a map on which one annotates the different sounds that one may encounter in wandering through a territory.

On a sheet of paper, create a map of your apartment, your campus, a coffee shop, or any other place and try to identify, in wandering around, what are the sounds that you can hear when you are positioned in a specific spot. Identify the surface occupied by the sound on the map. Can you hear the sound in the whole area? Is it limited to a specific place? What are the different sounds that mingle together when you move around? Pay attention to all of the sounds that you can find in a place, close your eyes, and focus on one of them at the time; identify it, locate it, and write a short description of it on the map (e.g., fridge, cars from road, birds, furnace, radio, TV set, snoring, etc.). You might come up with a map showing messy interminglings of sound, giving a sense of cacophony.[8] This is normal. The exercise's main objective is to force you to focus on sounds in trying to hear them and identify them. You might discover sounds in your apartment that you never heard before. You might also realize how we underestimate the complexity and presence of sounds in our environment; we often take sounds for granted.

Variation: Use a sound recording device and record each of the sounds that can be heard on your map. Recording a single sound at a time might be challenging, but it is a great exercise of focus and concentration. Develop a blog or a Google Earth project to create an interactive score of your soundwalk.[9] Take your friends on your soundwalk and have them listen to your recorded sounds. Can you still find the sounds you recorded at the same spot and with the same intensity? Ask your friends to add sounds to your map. They might hear sounds that you missed. Discuss your perception of the recorded sounds and the "live" ones. Do you feel a difference? Ask your friends to share their impressions.

Additional Resources

Sound Recordings

Feld, Steven (producer and recorder). 2001. *Bosavi: Rainforest Music from Papua New Guinea*. Smithsonian Folkways SFW 40487–2001.

Feld, Steven (recorder, editor, and photographer), and Mickey Hart (producer). 1991. *Voices of the Rainforest*. Smithsonian Folkways HRT 15009.

Turnbull, Colin M. (recorder), and Anne MacKaye Chapman (producer). 1992. *Mbuti Pygmies of the Ituri Rainforest*. Smithsonian Folkways SFW 40401.

Documentaries

New, David, dir. 2009. *Listen*. National Film Board of Canada. www.nfb.ca/film/listen

Riedelsheimer, Thomas, dir. 2004. *Touch the Sound: A Sound Journey with Evelyn Glennie*.

Rossato-Bennett, Michael, dir. 2014. *Alive Inside*. Projector Media.

Castaing-Taylor, Lucien, and Véréna Paravel, dirs. 2012. *Leviathan*. Also see the special issue of *Visual Anthropology Review*, vol. 31, no. 1 (2015), about this film.

Fiction Film

Simonsson, Ola, and Johannes Stjärne Nilsson, dirs. 2010. *Sound of Noise.*
    Bliss, Dfm Fiktion.

Websites

Sound blog, Centre for Imaginative Ethnography
    http://imaginativeethnography.org/soundings
Cities and Memory
    http://citiesandmemory.com/what-is-cities-and-memory-about
Saadiyat Soundscapes: Soundscapes of New York University Abu Dhabi
    campus produced by students
    http://nyuadsounds.info
Soundcities: A global soundmap project
    www.soundcities.com
Speaking maps
    www.speakingmaps.co.uk
Sensory Ethnography Lab
    https://sel.fas.harvard.edu
Centre for Sensory Studies
    www.centreforsensorystudies.org/member/david-howes
Sound Studies Laboratory
    www.soundstudieslab.org
Sound Ethnography Project
    http://soundethnography.com
Freesound
    www.freesound.org

References

Banks, Marcus, and Howard Morphy, eds. 1997. *Rethinking Visual Anthropology.* New
    Haven, CT:Yale University Press.
Barbash, Ilisa, and Lucien Taylor. 1997. *Cross-Cultural Filmmaking: A Handbook for Making
    Documentary and Ethnographic Films and Videos.* Berkeley: University of California
    Press.
Boudreault-Fournier, Alexandrine. 2012. "Écho d'une rencontre virtuelle: Vers une
    ethnographie de la production audio-visuelle." *Anthropologica* 54 (1): 1–12.
Boudreault-Fournier, Alexandrine. 2016. "Microtopia in Counterpoint: Relational
    Aesthetics and the Echo Project." *Cadernos de Arte e Antropologia* 5 (1): 135–54.

Boudreault-Fournier, Alexandrine, and Nick Wees. Forthcoming. "Creative Engagement with Interstitial Urban Spaces: The Case of Vancouver's Back Alley." In *Urban Encounters: Art and the Public*, eds. Martha Radice and Alexandrine Boudreault-Fournier. Montreal: McGill University Press.

Chion, Michel. 1994. *Audio-Vision: Sound on Screen*. New York: Columbia University Press.

Chion, Michel. 2003. *Un art sonore, le cinéma*. Paris: Cahiers du cinéma.

Clifford, James, and George E. Marcus. 1986. *Writing Culture: The Poetics and Politics of Ethnography*. Berkeley: University of California Press.

Drever, John Levack. 2002. "Soundscape Composition: The Convergence of Ethnography and Acousmatic Music." *Organised Sound* 7 (1): 21–7.

Fabian, Johannes. 1983. *Time and the Other: How Anthropology Makes Its Object*. New York: Columbia University Press.

Gardner, Robert, and Ákos Östör. 2001. *Making Forest of Bliss: Intention, Circumstance, and Chance in Nonfiction Film*. Cambridge, MA: Harvard University Press.

Grossman, Alyssa. 2013. "Filming in the Light of Memory." In *Transcultural Montage*, eds. Christian Suhr and Rane Willerslev, 198–212. New York: Berghahn.

Henley, Paul. 2007a. "Beyond the Burden of the Burden of the Real: An Anthropologist's Reflections on the Technique of 'A Masterful Cutter.'" In *The Cinema of Robert Gardner*, eds. Ilisa Barbash and Lucien Taylor, 33–57. Oxford: Berg.

Henley, Paul. 2007b. "Seeing, Hearing, Feeling: Sound and the Despotism of the Eye in 'Visual' Anthropology." *Visual Anthropology Review* 23 (1): 54–63. http://dx.doi.org/10.1525/var.2007.23.1.54

Hockings, Paul, ed. 2003. *Principles of Visual Anthropology*. Berlin: Mouton de Gruyter.

Ingold, Tim. 2000. *The Perception of the Environment: Essays on Livelihood, Dwelling and Skill*. London: Routledge. http://dx.doi.org/10.4324/9780203466025

Ingold, Tim. 2013. *Making: Anthropology, Archaeology, Art and Architecture*. London: Routledge.

Iscen, Ozgun Eylul. 2014. "In-Between Soundscapes of Vancouver: The Newcomer's Acoustic Experience of a City with a Sensory Repertoire of Another Place." *Organised Sound* 19 (2): 125–35. http://dx.doi.org/10.1017/S1355771814000065

Labelle, Brandon. 2011. *Acoustic Territories: Sound Culture and Everyday Life*. New York: Continuum.

MacDougall, David. 2006. *The Corporeal Image: Film, Ethnography, and the Senses*. Princeton, NJ: Princeton University Press.

MacDougall, David. 2009. "Anthropology and the Cinematic Imagination." In *Photography, Anthropology and History*, eds. Christopher Morton and Elizabeth Edwards, 55–65. Burlington, VT: Ashgate.

Marcus, George E. 1990. "The Modernist Sensibility in Recent Ethnographic Writing and the Cinematic Metaphor of Montage." *Visual Anthropology Review* 6 (1): 2–12. http://dx.doi.org/10.1525/var.1990.6.1.2

Marcus, George E. 2013. "Afterword: The Traffic in Montage, Then and Now." In *Transcultural Montage*, eds. Christian Suhr and Rane Willerslev, 302–7. New York: Berghahn.

Marcus, George, and Jay Ruby. 2011. "Introduction: Made to Be Seen Historical Perspectives on Visual Anthropology." In *Made to Be Seen: Perspectives on the History of Visual Anthropology*, eds. Marcus Banks and Jay Ruby, 1–18. Chicago: University of Chicago Press.

Mead, Margaret. [1974] 2003. "Visual Anthropology in a Discipline of Words." In *Principles of Visual Anthropology*, 3rd ed., ed. Paul Hockings, 3–11. Berlin: Mouton de Gruyter.

Pink, Sarah. 2001. *Doing Visual Ethnography*. London: Sage.

Pink, Sarah. 2009. *Doing Sensory Ethnography*. Los Angeles: Sage.

Ruby, Jay. 2000. *Picturing Culture: Explorations of Film and Anthropology*. Chicago: University of Chicago Press.

Schafer, R. Murray. [1977] 1994. *The Soundscape: Our Sonic Environment and the Tuning of the World*. Rochester, NY: Destiny Books.

Schneider, Arnd, and Christopher Wright. 2013a. "Ways of Working." In *Anthropology and Art Practice*, eds. Arnd Schneider and Christopher Wright, 1–24. London: Bloomsbury.

Schneider, Arnd, and Christopher Wright, eds. 2013b. *Anthropology and Art Practice*. London: Bloomsbury.

Schneider, Arnd, and Caterina Pasqualino, eds. 2014. *Experimental Film and Anthropology*. London: Bloomsbury.

Sterne, Jonathan. 2003. *The Audible Past: Cultural Origins of Sound Reproduction*. Durham, NC: Duke University Press. http://dx.doi.org/10.1215/9780822384250

Sterne, Jonathan. 2012. "Sonic Imaginations." In *The Sound Studies Reader*, ed. Jonathan Sterne, 1–17. London: Routledge.

Sullivan, Graeme. 2010. *Art Practice as Research: Inquiry in Visual Arts*. 2nd ed. Thousand Oaks, CA: Sage.

Truax, Barry. 2001. *Acoustic Communication*. London: Ablex.

Truax, Barry. 2012. "Sound, Listening and Place: The Aesthetic Dilemma." *Organised Sound* 17 (3): 193–201. http://dx.doi.org/10.1017/S1355771811000380

Westerkamp, Hildegard. 2002. "Linking Soundscape Composition and Acoustic Ecology." *Organised Sound* 7 (1): 51–6. http://dx.doi.org/10.1017/S1355771802001085

Willerslev, Rane, and Christian Suhr. 2013. "Introduction: Montage as an Amplifier of Invisibility." In *Transcultural Montage*, eds. Christian Suhr and Rane Willerslev, 1–16. New York: Berghahn.

Filmography

Gardner, Robert, dir. 1986. *Forest of Bliss*. Documentary Educational Resources.

Grossman, Alyssa, dir. 2010. Lumina *Amintirri (In The Light of Memory)*. Granada Centre for Visual Anthropology, University of Manchester.

Hitchcock, Alfred, dir. 1960. *Psycho.* Paramount Pictures.

Holström, Lasse, dir. 2000. *Chocolat.* Miramax Films.

Sherman, Nick, dir. 2010. *Soundtracker..* FouFilms.

Tarentino, Quentin, dir. 1997. *Jackie Brown.* Miramax Films.

Tarentino, Quentin, dir. 2003/2004. *Kill Bill.* Miramax Films.

Sound Documentary

Jones, Lealan, and Lloyd Newman in collaboration with David Isay. 1993. *Ghetto Life 101.* Soundportraits.org

Notes

1 Also, as mentioned by Willerslev and Suhr, the term "montage" in French refers to "the technical process of film editing in the strict sense of the word" (2013, 6).

2 The film can be watched at www.youtube.com/watch?v=otVuU37JqmI

3 The sound documentary was produced by Soundportraits.org and is available at http://soundportraits.org/on-air/ghetto_life_101

4 For further discussion of this process and how it can be applied to innovative approaches to audio-visual anthropology, see Boudreault-Fournier and Wees (forthcoming).

5 See the clip "Soundscape and Videoscape—Back Alley Vancouver" at https://vimeo.com/78777150

6 See the clip "Acoustic of a Saxophone Player in Vancouver's Back Alley" at https://vimeo.com/73407966

7 See the clip "Football Game in Cidade Tiradentes—World Cup 2014" at https://vimeo.com/107946581. The clip was produced in collaboration with Rose Satiko Hikiji and Sylvia Caiuby Novaes.

8 For example, see the Jerusalem soundmap by the designer Roni Levit (http://visual.ly/jerusalem-sound-map).

9 For example, visit the Saadiyat Soundscapes project, which consists of soundscapes recorded by students of the New York University Abu Dhabi campus (http://nyuadsounds.info).

CHAPTER 5

WALKING

Cristina Moretti

IMAGE 5.1: Community chessboard and park.
Public space as an invitation to dwell and to meet others:
a community-created park with benches, a bulletin
board, a free library, and giant pieces for playing chess
and checkers, Vancouver, Canada.

Credit: Cristina Moretti, 2016.

Read this chapter on the bus. Or on a park bench. Or while waiting for a street performer, a protest rally, or a festival to begin. What do you notice around you? Who is in this place with you, and why do you think they are there? Would you call this a "public space," and why? If you are sitting on a bench, your questions can even start from this ordinary, everyday piece of street furniture. Who is welcome to use it, and who is discouraged from lingering here? Is your bench divided into sections, to prevent people from sleeping on it at night? Giulio Iacchetti, an Italian designer, provocatively created a "day and night bench" which can be turned upside down at the end of the day to provide a shelter.[1] Iacchetti's multipurpose object is an indirect critique: If public space is supposed to belong to everyone, why are people not allowed to sleep and loiter in parks, and why are the homeless among the most marginalized, medicalized, and controlled city inhabitants (Lyon-Callo 2008)?

Another provocation comes in the form of "Pay and Sit," an installation by German photographer Fabian Brunsing.[2] A video of the installation shows a bench that works like a meter: its sharp retractable teeth lower into their grooves once a coin is inserted, but rise up again when the purchased time has elapsed, making it impossible to continue sitting. Brunsing imagines a possible future in which only the wealthy will be able to enjoy sitting in a park. What if this were the case now? Would you be sitting here or somewhere else? Brunsing focuses on a single element—the bench—but his critique refers to public space more broadly. How are plazas and parks increasingly geared toward the affluent? In which ways has public space already been seized, commodified, and privatized, as Low and Smith (2006) decry? And what are the consequences if public space is increasingly understood as a good available only to those who can afford it?

Although observing who uses, inhabits, and claims certain spaces helps illuminate social relations in both cities and rural environments, urban public spaces have received particular attention by contemporary scholars. For one, the density and heterogeneity of urban life renders plazas, streets, and parks into arenas of conflicts, negotiations, and actions toward social change. For the other, central urban plazas and streets are often invested with symbolic and representational power, thus embodying authority and allowing for its questioning by regular inhabitants. For these reasons, anthropologists have been interested in how public space can help foster political, cultural, and social engagement. Thinking along those lines, several individuals and groups have proposed benches that encourage interaction between strangers. For example, a swinging bench showcased by the organization Esterni[3] during its 2009 Public Design Festival in Milan, Italy, features a round base that accommodates up to six people. Its occupants face each other and can make the bench swing by coordinating the movement of their bodies, playfully suggesting that public space can and should encourage conversations and collaborations between city dwellers.

These diverse kinds of benches—and many more could be added—harness our imagination in order for us to question the social relations in the communities we live in. Similarly, in what follows, I encourage you to use public space as a location, a starting point, a question, and an idea—shared as well as contested—to imagine what our society could be like and to attend to other inhabitants' imaginative practices. These include the stories, movements, and performances through which residents relate to each other, create a sense of place, and engage with public space as a site of belonging, identity, difference, and/or conflict.

In this chapter, I suggest possible directions and questions for research, starting from the ordinary activity of walking as an ethnographic strategy. Leave the actual or metaphorical park bench where you have been sitting, and begin walking in your community. What will you notice and who will you meet? How are your routes, the way you move (see, for example, Truitt 2008), and your encounters shaped by your social position and identities? How does the very act of journeying help you claim a place in the larger society or in your community? How do you, through your itinerary, become part of the landscape, a strand in the spider web of bodies, sounds, and daily performances? As a way of inhabiting, researching, and representing everyday realities, walking is an imaginative practice. It helps us learn to see, imagine, and understand public spaces and other rural/suburban/urban locales from the particular perspectives and social positions of those we journey with. This means not just moving through existent spaces and realities but also following what different inhabitants imagine and remember (Irving 2010), what they miss and strive for (Schielke 2012), and the critical connections they draw between people, places, and stories.

I am using an expanded concept of public space in this chapter. I think of it as a rather unstable category, both an idea and a set of actual places that acquire meaning as people use, narrate, journey through, and comment on them. To say it simply, public space likely means something different to you than it does to other people. Do public schools and libraries count as public spaces? What about subways and buses? Are women's centers or alternative, politically active associations public spaces? Or perhaps public space is less a particular site than a momentary position, from which people, as critical agents, can comment on and attempt to change society? Instead of assuming that public space is a shared and easily defined category with obvious functions, it is much more productive to research the relations and practices through which people understand something as public space, and through which they actively create particular kinds of places and identities (Moretti 2015; see also Butler 2011). I understand public space as both an object of research and a dynamic, embodied site of inquiry, interaction, imagination, and engagement. Rather than assume that any meaning of public space is fixed, my research process takes unforeseen connections, detours, and interruptions as a source of insights. All of these can be opportunities for engaging with the imaginative practices involved in thinking about, constructing, using, and inhabiting the communities we live in.

In suggesting these paths for research, I take inspiration from urban anthropologists' work, as well as from the ideas of ethnographers who have studied walking as a research strategy, a practice of learning, and a way of being in place. Urban scholars' interest in public space emerges in large part from a concern that contemporary cities are becoming more unequal and fragmented. They ask, Could accessible, lively, and welcoming public spaces help create communities that are more just and conducive to an active and critical participatory democracy? How, on the contrary, are everyday engagements with public space part of processes of marginalization and discrimination?

To this end, inhabitants, activists, and scholars have been interested in both the idea and everyday lives of urban public spaces. Plazas, streets, and parks can be used for a variety of purposes by many different "publics"; this flexibility emphasizes "ideals of openness and accessibility both in the city space and in the polity" (Caldeira 2000, 298). The notion of public space as open and accessible to everyone, irrespective of gender, race, class, citizenship, age, sexuality, ability, and more, is an important mobilizing idea for groups and individuals seeking to gain recognition (Mitchell 1995). Public spaces, as material and symbolic locations, allow groups to be seen and to claim a place in society, and potentially, to trouble existing ideas and relations. The Occupy movement in various cities (see, for example, Juris and Razsa 2011), and the 2011 events in Tahrir Square in Cairo, Egypt, are good examples of how public space can create visibility for a group or an idea. If you have ever participated in a demonstration, you can probably relate to this aspect firsthand.

While all of this speaks to the positive, even ideal, roles of public spaces, anthropologists are concerned with how urban streets, plazas, and parks can also be sites of discrimination, exclusion, and control. Lower-income residents, Indigenous people, visible minority inhabitants, and immigrants are among those who are often stopped by police or prevented in subtle and not-so-subtle ways from using and congregating in public spaces (Holston and Appadurai 1999). They are often seen as belonging to other areas of the city (Razack 2000), as threatening the decor or historical identity of a neighborhood (Dines 2002), or as presenting a danger to public security.

Gender and sexuality are other important axes of exclusion in contemporary cities (Guano 2007; Pratt 1988). Because of these complex problems and possibilities, doing research on and in public space can be a productive way to examine inequality and shifting social relations and to trace how individuals and groups resist oppression, propose new ideas, and negotiate their roles in their communities. While urban anthropologists have focused such questions on the cityscape, we can ask similar questions of the public spaces located in rural contexts, whether they are national parks or children's playgrounds.

Studying public space is also interesting because it opens wider questions on how to examine performative engagements in social space (Fikes 2009; Guano 2002). Appearing and circulating in public spaces entails negotiating one's identity and place in the world. As an embodied, social, and imaginary practice, walking can be a way of telling, commenting on, performing, and creating both stories and places. This requires us to pay attention to imagination as it helps generate understandings, connections, and questions. To make matters more complicated, Vigh reminds us that when people move, they often do so in a space that is itself constantly shifting (see also Archambault 2013). Walking is then more akin to "navigating": "moving within a moving environment" that is "always emergent and unfolding" (Vigh 2009, 424, 425). Walking in public spaces thus involves multiple dimensions; it means engaging with the social space as it is, as it might be, and as it could be. Using Vigh's words, we need to be "constantly attuned both to the way we move in the here and now as well as to the way we move in relation to social goals and prospective positions. In this manner, navigation is, importantly, related to movement through both the socially *immediate* and the socially *imagined*. It designates the complex of actions and interpretations that enable one to act in the here and now, gain an idea of the possible routes and courses that emerge from the present and direct one's movement expediently toward possible futures" (Vigh 2009, 425–26).

While in this chapter I focus on walking in and researching cities, the ideas and methods suggested can be useful in rural or remote contexts as well. Tuck-Po (2008), for example, emphasizes the links between stories and walking itineraries in the forests of Malaysia. Moving with Batek hunter-gatherers enables Tuck-Po to reflect on the ethnographer's position and on walking as a way of negotiating social connections. Walking is also a way to connect the past and the present to validate and re-establish relations to ancestors or past events (Walsh 2012; Legat 2008; Lund 2008; Basso 1996). In any setting—a remote forest, deserted seashore, suburban cul-de-sac, or metropolitan streetscape—walking with others can help us appreciate people's senses of place while urging us to reflect on the social relations that shape them.

Walking Itineraries

During my fieldwork in Milan, Italy, I decided that I would start learning about the role of public space by asking different inhabitants to guide me, on foot, through their city. I chose this method because I wanted a research practice that was open-ended enough for me to follow my guides' ideas, memories, and explanatory frameworks and that took into consideration people's embodied, sensual participation in city life (see also Pink 2008). Walking meant following the perfume of freshly baked bread and roasting chestnuts, responding to bitterly cold mornings with childhood memories of icicles, and entering shops to leaf through old books. As de Certeau (1984) described, moreover, the improvisational character of walking helps us attend to people's itineraries as a lived relationship with a city, a connection that continually changes.

Following people's itineraries as a research method has received increasing attention in the past few years (see, for example, Irving 2010; Ingold and Vergunst 2008; Pink 2008; and Guano 2003). Walking tours are particularly interesting for the ethnographer because they do much more than reveal a series of places, memories, and relations that are simply and already "there." They open a performative space: a time and place for inhabitants to take on, bend, and respond to the many histories, questions, and meanings that might be associated to particular locales. When I started my fieldwork in Milan, for example, I assumed that the most important insight I could gain through this methodology would be which public spaces my interlocutors valued and used. Without realizing it, I expected that my guides would point me to existing plazas, streets, or buildings, and "explain" them to me. Soon, however, I found myself bewildered and inspired by their responses. For one, several interlocutors situated themselves along discordant borders between cultures, times, or social realities. They showed me both how they belonged to the city (e.g., by claiming that they knew intimately the history of a particular place) and, at the same time, how they felt they were treading its margins (e.g., by criticizing recent changes or by struggling to find places, people, and stories that spoke to their experience). Many of my guides also talked about what was not there, speaking instead about what they imagined, remembered, suspected, or wished were there. An example of this was the water: Milan does not have a lake, coast, or significant river, and many of its Navigli canals were covered by streets in the 1930s. The missing water, surprisingly, became part of many discussions on Milan's public spaces. Some respondents wondered what Milan would be like if it had a beach. One middle-aged woman talked about the possibility of water rising and submerging parts of the city—not just because there have been a few instances of the rising water table affecting the subway and underground garages, but more importantly as a powerful metaphor of how Milan's industrial past may come to haunt the post-industrial city.

These complicated responses were about much more than public space, spurring me to follow the intricate connections and disconnections that my interlocutors saw operating in their city. They were also political: the people I met talked about public space to criticize inequality, neoliberalism, the marginalization of immigrants, and the difficulty of obtaining affordable housing (Moretti 2015). The guided walks were both thematic and experiential, as public space was not only something that we could talk about but also something we could experience together: an embodied, shared, and collaboratively constructed reality where our journey took place. As such, the walks directed my attention not just to the object but also to the process of research. How did my guides and I construct an itinerary together? What kind of audience was I for them, and how did this shape our conversations? What did I learn from their ways of understanding, interpreting, and representing the spaces they inhabit, and how would this shape my ethnographic practices? What kind of knowledge were we creating together, and for which purpose?

If you intend to use guided walking tours in your research, the following are some suggestions to get you started.

Think of Guided Walks as a Shared Performative Practice

Walking, as Liisa Malkki (2007, 178) says about ethnography, is "a way of being in the world." When we go for a walk, our directions, journeys, and encounters are shaped by what we can do and who we can be on those streets (Pratt 1988). In turn, being and moving through space helps us construct our identities for ourselves and for others, and to claim, literally and metaphorically, a space in the world. As Maggie O'Neill and Phil Hubbard (2010, 56) point out, "walking is itself never simply about traversing a route from one place to another: the journey itself is performative, an act of place-making and an active engagement with the environment." During ethnographic walks, you and your guide will not only visit certain landmarks together; you will perform certain itineraries, modes of listening and seeing, as well as ways of relating to each other and to the spaces around you. This, moreover, will take place in a wider context, where complex performative negotiations are often central to processes of exclusion and belonging (Goldstein 2010; Partridge 2008; Fikes 2009; Fleetwood 2004). You may want to ask, How do my guides and I enact being an inhabitant of this space at this time and place? Which practices might inform this walk? What knowledge of the city are my guides showing and/or relying upon, and how is this constituted? How does this speak to other ways of being and moving in the city? What else could my guides show me, and why were these paths chosen?

For all my interlocutors, guiding me through the city involved acting as a knowledgeable inhabitant, yet it differed greatly in how this knowledge and their linkages to the city were defined, how they were expressed, and how they shaped our walk and our movements through the streets. Whereas one of my guides directed my gaze to particular landmarks and showed her familiarity with Milan through her way of seeing and apprehending the landscape, others led me through the city as if it were a maze, urging me to notice the underlying connections between people, spaces, and stories. An elderly Italian-born woman met me in the center of town because this is where she worked when she was younger, and she introduced me a store that was an important resource for seamstresses of her generation, thus showing her connection to practices and identities that are now largely displaced by the current fashion industry. Another one of my guides brought me to a historical palace to explain how it belonged to her family in the past and thus to trace her linkages to some of the oldest Milanese families.

For some of my interlocutors who had recently migrated to Milan from other countries, acting as a knowledgeable guide was a way to show that they belonged to the city. Two migrant women who worked as nannies and caretakers, for example, brought me to see some of Milan's art to affirm that they did actively participate in the cultural and social life of the city, even if many Italian-born inhabitants refuted that claim. For all of these guides, what they could tell me about Milan was a way of showing me what kinds of inhabitants they were and how they positioned themselves within a community. Their stories, moreover, were not just a commentary; they were moving, situational, social engagements with place.

Because you and your interlocutors will create a dynamic, embodied, and, at least to a certain extent, improvisational itinerary together, it is crucial that you think carefully about how you will negotiate your roles, the purpose of the project, and its end results. Who will you ask to lead you? Why and how will they want to be involved? How will ethics, accountability, and responsibility inform your journeys? You might want to consider, for example, using Dara Culhane's three-part consent process, in which research participants agree to be involved in a project one phase at a time, and decide during the research process rather than beforehand what the product of their meetings will look like (for a full description of this method, see Culhane 2011).[4]

Another thing to consider when planning your walking tours is how you will record your itinerary (the routes, commentaries, movements through the city, and engagements with people and places that your guides will lead you through) and how this will affect your journey (see Alexandrine Boudreault-Fournier's chapter, "Recording and Editing," in this volume). An interesting difference among the city walks was my guides' involvement in photographing the tour. Some of them took a very active role, instructing me where and how to take pictures and video recordings of the places they were showing me. This affirmed their role as teachers and mine as learner or apprentice. Other guides, however, took pictures or videos themselves, because they wanted to document their city. Following their practices with my camera—and noticing what they photographed or recorded, how, and why—helped me to see the city through their eyes. Lastly, another guide was pleased that I had a camera with me and could take photographs of the city for her to send to her family and friends. These were not just different ways of documenting an itinerary; they reflected and shaped the different meanings that my interlocutors gave to the walks and the reasons they decided to guide me.

But you can also record your walks by focusing on sounds. Andrew Irving focuses not on visual recordings but on recording dialogues and inner reverie (our thoughts made public by talking out loud) in his New York Stories project[5] (Irving 2015). Attention to listening and recording what you hear while walking could work in any number of spaces. What soundscapes do you hear in your rural, urban, suburban spaces? Consider creating a sonic ethnography recording of your walking tour using a digital recorder, smartphone, or a combined visual–audio recorder. What do you hear listening to the recording that you missed while walking? Do you hear the train, a plane overhead, Canada geese cries, a distant horn, the wind blowing, a child humming, a busker performing, a street-corner sermon, or your own voice? Also ask yourself what sounds you do not hear as you walk. Perhaps your cityscape prevents you from hearing the birds chirp or the rivers flow; or your rural landscape lacks the bangs, shouts, and sirens of the city. As an example, see Steven Feld's "Voices of the Rainforest," which blends together the sounds of everyday life with the music of the Kaluli people in Papua New Guinea to represent the overlapping and layered effects of soundscapes (Feld 1990). You can hear the grass being cut, birdsongs by the creek, insects in the air, and the voices in community dialogues.

Think of Guided Walks as a Practice of Co-Imagining

Walking tours are exercises in the imagination. The latter is integral to ethnography, because it helps us envision different explanations and points of view and because through ethnography we are called to respond to the imaginative practices of the people we work with (see, for example, Schielke 2013 and Navaro-Yashin 2009).

Asking people to be our walking guides means to invite local residents to imagine their routes and, in turn, for us to respond to their imagined spaces. Imagining here refers not to a detachment from reality, but rather to a complex engagement with it (Appadurai 1996). Imagining can be a way of inhabiting the

landscape, thinking of the past and the future, or engaging in collective projects. Imagination is also central to living with hopeful possibilities of a more
just society (Dolan 2005). During my research, for example, my guides often
imagined the lives of other inhabitants, asking, "How do people other than
me live in Milan?" Some key questions in this respect are, How do particular
ideas and imaginative practices reinforce or maintain structures of domination
and oppression? How do they challenge and reframe hegemonic structures
and power relations? How do memories and longing get attached to particular places in ways that are simultaneously ephemeral, situated, and always
connected to other stories?

One afternoon, I met a group of youth who were dancing on the platform
of a subway station. During our conversation, they asked me to take a picture
of them, instructing me very precisely as to how I should photograph them
to capture the right shape and combination of their moves. Their insistence
that I look at their group and movements in a very particular way struck me.
I realized that I was asked to imagine with them that this was a dance floor
rather than a subway station. This was important for them, because as Latin
American youth in Milan they were often singled out as "different" and criticized as those who made "wrong" or "unconventional" uses of city spaces—like
holding dances in the subway (Moretti 2015). But if this were a dance floor,
what could be peculiar about their gathering and dancing there?

Walking tours help us to attune to how inhabitants imagine in and through
city spaces. More to the point, following our interlocutors to locations that are
significant to them can be understood as a practice of co-imagining. As in the
example above, we are not only listening to our guides' stories or comments;
we are asked to participate in particular ways of inhabiting and understanding
the city. When an elderly guide walked me along the buildings from which,
as a child, she would collect icicles on the way to school, she was inviting me
to imagine holding those glistening treasures with her and to imagine what
it felt like to grow up in a working-class neighborhood, among hardships and
promises, just after World War II.

"Co-imagining" thus means to follow not just your guides' footsteps but
their ideas, memories, and strategies for understanding. How do they theorize the city? What will your research and arguments look like if you follow
their local theories and explanatory frameworks (Tsing 1993, 31)? What are the
stakes? What are the consequences of their critiques? What other possibilities
for living and learning are you invited to imagine together with your interlocutors? This is more than simply witnessing or listening to the suggestions,
stories, or explanations of the people we walk with,[6] as their ways of imagining the city invite us to both question and reframe what we want to know,
why we want to know it, and what the effects of that knowledge may be.

Through the shared, embodied practice of walking we are called to re-imagine our ethnographic work and insights, starting from our interlocutors' ways of interrogating and apprehending. The embodied, reflexive practice of walking with our interlocutors becomes a methodology: as Tsing writes (1993, 225), their "situated," "critical . . . ethnography makes [ours] possible."

During my research, for example, there were different ways to understand what public space was. Some of the people I met criticized the very use of the term: oppositional, independent social centers suggested that public space is a fiction, because all space is appropriated by powerful interests—only actively claimed and "liberated" spaces that are conducive to political action are to be called or considered public spaces (Moretti 2015). This perspective challenged the very ways I was thinking about the city and its spaces, suggesting that ethnography "bend" or even deconstruct the definition of public space to problematize who is included and excluded in the societies where we work and live. And their practices of "squatting" (illegally occupying and using) abandoned buildings to convert them into community centers proposed that public spaces are those that meddle with the very distinctions between public and private, questioning the very way ownership, belonging, and power are organized and distributed in an urban community. This also made me think about the places where knowledge is constructed and shared. If, as many of my interlocutors claimed, learning and understanding are best done while walking on the city's streets, and while other lives touch ours through chance encounters and everyday movements, would a performed, walking ethnography be better suited to representing a city than a written document?

Think of Guided Walks as an Ethnographic Method Enabled by Interruptions

Walking tours are often filled with interruptions: there might be surprise encounters and dialogues along the way, detours to be taken; street performers, birdsongs, and children's cries to listen to; decaying and rotting smells to avoid; and speeding bicycle carriers, street cars, or wild bears to run from (for a walking tour based on sound, and offering surprises, see Rosenblum 2013). Your guides might spend time looking for a particular site that is difficult to find, getting lost on the way, or discovering places they had not anticipated seeing. While we can cast aside interruptions and surprises, focusing only on what we intend to see, explain, or learn about, such interruptions and detours can offer crucial insights. It is exactly the ephemeral, improvisational practice of inhabiting space, which involves being confronted with unanticipated ideas and relations, that is so vital to public space and everyday life. More to the point, interruptions and surprises are not an unavoidable by-product but rather a key advantage in ethnographic research (Malkki 2007, 174): they allow us to move beyond received paradigms, to confront assumptions, and to gain new experiences and understandings. These help us become attuned to the lived perspectives of our interlocutors and rethink the social realities we encounter.

Lastly, Think of Research Itself as a Walking Tour

Ethnography is an embodied practice of learning in the presence of others. It is always partial, as we choose routes through our spaces and specific questions to guide us. Our itinerary allows us to perceive and experience connections between particular realities, ideas, and groups of people, which are often best seen from the streets, dirt roads, or abandoned paths and in the everyday life of inhabitants. Reflecting on why we see these linkages and from which standpoints can help us pay attention to how particular realities and systems leave traces in the city and other landscapes, and how different inhabitants come across them, in particular, situated, embodied ways. In Kalimantan, Indonesia, Tsing (2005, 176–77) relates learning about the difficulty of distinguishing "between familiar categories of 'cultivated' and 'wild'" by sitting in people's homes, eating fruits, and tossing "the seeds out the door." Harms (2010, 89), researching urbanization in Vietnam's Ho Chi Minh City, describes learning about the city's edges while traveling from one urban district to another while sitting on the back of a motorcycle, "amid the rumbling thunder of passing trucks, the sounding of air horns on the half-finished highway, and the whipping wind of our own motion across the landscape." Where will you be sitting, standing, or moving when you build your insights and encounter new ideas? What will you miss and which unique perspectives will you encounter?

Imagining Traces and Absences

The water was not the only thing whose absence was felt during my research in Milan. Consider this incident from my field notes:

> Today I met an older woman on the bus. After commenting on some of the changes in Milan in the past decades, the woman explained that she used to be a seamstress. "We seamstresses are like white flies, you know?" she said. "White flies?" I asked. "Yes, there are no more of us!" she answered. I replied, smiling: "All the seamstresses I meet are telling me that they are all gone, but I keep meeting them!" In fact, the woman on the bus is the third "white fly" I have encountered by chance in the last ten days! (28 May 2011)

Conversations and encounters like this one yield small, oblique commentaries. Yet they might be less irrelevant than they seem. A few days before the bus conversation, I had met another seamstress, Renata, who similarly said that people like her did not exist anymore—yet there we were, walking and talking along streets and piazzas. Why did Renata and the woman on the bus position themselves as those who were no longer there? In our conversation, Renata told me about living on a limited income in a social housing complex where conditions were poor. Her explanation about the network of tailors and seamstresses that disappeared was also a reflection on inequality, and on the sweeping social changes she has experienced as an inhabitant of Milan. Just a week earlier, I had walked through the city with another elderly seamstress as my guide. Stopping in front of a field left vacant by deindustrialization, she described how "the hems—of skirts, of all clothing—are now terribly made." What was I to do with those rough edges, the fabric of spaces, lives, and stories that were coming undone? How was I to write about them? My interlocutors' responses voiced some of the disjunctures they felt as low-income women in the city: being people "no longer there" reflected a more widespread sense of changing place (see Moretti 2015, 2011).

If you are carrying out research in public space, you might stumble upon similar uncertain traces, oblique comments, and jarring associations. You could call them, as Avery Gordon (1997) does, "ghostly matters"—those people, objects, places, and connections that are supposedly no longer there, and, because of this, "haunt" social reality. Gordon's ghosts are akin to ruins, zones of disrepair, invisible places, or interstices (Chu 2014; Navaro-Yashin 2009; Tonnelat 2008), as they all can unsettle categories or emerge as ambivalent, contradictory locations. Sometimes these ghostly spaces can be seen as a particular kind of public space, though maybe often not recognized as such, because they are marginal, in flux, or at the edge of things. But as sites on the edge, in flux, or at the margins, they may provide room for conversations, engagement, or interrogations, because they can offer different associations or points of view than the ones we are used to. In this way, they can help us to critically reevaluate our very ways of knowing.

Gordon's (1997, 17) call to notice "how that which appears absent can indeed be a seething presence" is not intended to distract us from the systemic injustices and practices of exclusion taking place in the city. It is not the same as starting a research project without particular questions, theoretical orientations, or concerns in mind, just hoping to find something curious and unusual. On the contrary, because systems of oppression are often so pervasive, subtle, and contradictory, and can work by generating consensus rather than coercion, it becomes all the more important to listen for discordant voices, alternative visions of reality, or moments that suggest that things could be otherwise.

Intervening

IMAGE 5.2: "We are the ones we have been waiting for."
Writing on the sidewalk during an Earth Day climate justice demonstration
and festival, Vancouver, Canada.

Credit: Cristina Moretti, 2013.

Public space is a dynamic site of interventions. Public art, community projects, festivals, and political rallies all use public space as an avenue for cultural production, social commentary, and critical engagement. (We might subscribe to some of these projects, while being completely opposed to others.) Here I am thinking primarily of temporary installations, performances, or spaces, such as the mapping project El Tejido Urbano[7] and Park(ing) Day,[8] an annual international event during which metered parking spaces are temporarily transformed into installations or sites for social interaction.

One way to start a research project on public space—or to use public space to research particular topics or issues—is to follow, participate in, and respond to interventions and initiatives that you encounter in your urban community. What are the goals of these projects? Who participates and why? What role does public space play in these actions or installations? How do the aims and visions of these groups align with or depart from scholarly work? As these questions suggest, engaging ethnographically with interventions in public space can mean much more than studying an event, a movement, or a group. It can lead you to become a critical participant in one of these projects, involved in carefully thinking about the kinds of collaborations and alliances possible between anthropologists, activists, and artists (for examples, see Pink et al. 2010).

Doing so can be an opportunity to investigate different models for thinking, learning, representing, and participating in city life. Which orientations for research and action do these projects provide? How do they suggest we look at the city? What would or could happen if we incorporated these formats, styles, and modes of understanding and inquiring into ethnographic research and representation? These wide-ranging questions cause us to examine the relation between ethnography as a practice of learning and relating to the world and the site where it takes place (Moretti 2011). To what extent can ethnography be a kind of intervention, a "political process of knowledge recirculation" (Culhane 2011, 261)? If it can, what are its goals, and what is at stake? Which kinds of knowledges, ethical commitments, resources, and relations are required?

If you are interested in experimenting with these questions and ideas, you might want to try to design a project that takes place in public space. An inspiring example is the "re-speaking" initiative described by Julie Wyman (2009), which involves passersby reciting and performing historical speeches in Chicago parks. If you plan on creating or researching ethnographic interventions in your city, it is crucial that you think carefully about ethical implications: Who will you talk to and why? How will you take seriously their interests and concerns, and which relations will you establish? Who could be your allies? How will you seek collaborations with individuals, groups, organizations, or movements, and what role could you play in their projects? How will you ensure ethical relations with the people you will encounter? Think about the reasons why you would start the project: What are the social conditions, stories, or events you wish to understand and/or critique? What is at stake? What are some differences between such a project and an ethnography aimed at producing a paper or an article, and how will this inform the process and your relations with the people you work with?

Student Exercises

1. Walking Tours

Create a walking tour addressing a particular issue, topic, or phenomenon. Possible topics might include gentrification, public art and public space, activism, gendered spaces, poverty, cosmopolitanism, mobility, neoliberalism, and health and illness. You could also create a walking tour focused on a particular sense, such as smell, taste, or sound.

- Select five stations for your tour. For each station, include a photograph and explain at each of these stops what you would say as a guide.

Which comments would you offer at this location to the person you would be guiding? What would you like her or him to appreciate, understand, or consider about this place and your presence there?

- Draft a conclusion that summarizes your reflections on the tour as a whole. Which aspects are easy to explore through a walking tour, and which ones might be more difficult to notice or address?

If you wish to extend this assignment, these are two possibilities:

- While this exercise can take the form of a paper, you can experiment leading this tour for different people in your class. What happens? Do the conversations change? How does your understanding of the places you visit change?
- Think of ways to present this tour to your class, experimenting with different formats. Ideas can include a series of photographs, a video, a poster, a performance, or a double-faced paper quilt (with each square presenting a location, and each side of the square offering different comments or interpretation of this place).

2. **Noticing**

- Use a journal (include four to seven entries) or a photo essay to document particular objects, inscriptions, or events in public spaces that you find surprising, unruly, or inspiring, or that raise questions for you. Why do they catch your attention? What do they suggest about public space, urban life, or social inequality?
- Make a list of public spaces that you use in your everyday life. Why are they important to you? What do you value about them? How do other inhabitants use them, and what could this say about their lives and social positions?

Additional Resources

Websites
Egypt: The Songs of Tahrir Square. Music at the Heart of the Revolution
This web documentary by Hussein Emara and Priscille Lafitte about the 2011 Egyptian uprising allows you to journey to different locales in Cairo and explore some of the linkages between music, political action, and public space.
http://musictahrir.france24.com/tahrir-en.html
El Tejido Urbano
This mapping project by Liz Kueneke uses embroidered maps to encourage residents to discuss spaces in their urban communities. See the second link for videos of the project from different cities.

http://cargocollective.com/lizkueneke/The-Urban-Fabric-El-Tejido-Urbano

https://vimeo.com/lizkueneke/videos

European Prize for Urban Public Space

Organized by the Centre of Contemporary Culture of Barcelona, this site
and its archive document public space interventions in different European
cities, and its library offers texts and lectures on public space by scholars
from different disciplines.

www.publicspace.org/en

International Working Group on Public Space and Diversity

Among the resources of this site, coordinated by Setha Low and Darshan
Vigneswaran, is a bibliography on different aspects of public space.

www.mmg.mpg.de/subsites/public-space-and-diversity/homepage

Park(ing) Day

This site by Rebar documents and encourages participation in annual Park(ing)
Day events in various cities (usually the third Friday in September).

www.parkingday.org

Public Design Festival

This site documents Esterni's yearly festival in Milan, Italy, which transforms
parking sites into usable public spaces and installations.

www.publicdesignfestival.org/portal/EN/contents/generic_home.php?&

Urban Bricolage

This fun collection by Emile Hooge showcases playful ideas and do-it-yourself
interventions in public spaces.

http://urbanbricolage.tumblr.com

Vancouver Mural Tour

This site, sponsored by the City of Vancouver, offers an interesting example
of walking tours; it describes four itineraries in Vancouver focusing on
murals.

www.vancouvermurals.ca

References

Appadurai, Arjun. 1996. *Modernity at Large: Cultural Dimensions of Globalization.*
Minneapolis: University of Minnesota Press.

Archambault, Julie Soleil. 2013. "Cruising through Uncertainty: Cell Phones and the
Politics of Display and Disguise in Inhambane, Mozambique." *American Ethnologist*
40 (1): 88–101. http://dx.doi.org/10.1111/amet.12007

Basso, Keith. 1996. *Wisdom Sits in Places: Language and Landscape among the Western
Apache.* Albuquerque: University of New Mexico Press.

Butler, Judith. 2011. "Bodies in Alliance and the Politics of the Street." *Transversal: European Institute for Progressive Cultural Policies*, #Occupy and Assemble (October). http://eipcp.net/transversal/1011/butler/en

Caldeira, Teresa Pires do Rio. 2000. *City of Walls: Crime, Segregation, and Citizenship in São Paulo*. Berkeley: University of California Press.

Chu, Julie. 2014. "When Infrastructures Attack: The Workings of Disrepair in China." *American Ethnologist* 41 (2): 351–67. http://dx.doi.org/10.1111/amet.12080

Culhane, Dara. 2011. "Stories and Plays: Ethnography, Performance and Ethical Engagements." *Anthropologica*. Special Theme Issue: New Directions in Experimental and Engaged Ethnography 53 (2): 257–74.

de Certeau, Michel. 1984. *The Practice of Everyday Life*. Berkeley: University of California Press.

Dines, Nicholas. 2002. "Urban Renewal, Immigration, and Contested Claims to Public Space: The Case of Piazza Garibaldi in Naples." *GeoJournal* 58 (2/3): 177–88. http://dx.doi.org/10.1023/B:GEJO.0000010837.87618.59

Dolan, Jill. 2005. *Utopia in Performance: Finding Hope at the Theater*. Ann Arbor: University of Michigan Press.

Feld, Steven. 1990. *Sound and Sentiment: Birds, Weeping, Poetics, and Song in Kaluli Expression*. Philadelphia: University of Pennsylvania Press.

Fikes, Kesha. 2009. *Managing African Portugal: The Citizen-Migrant Distinction*. Durham, NC: Duke University Press. http://dx.doi.org/10.1215/9780822390985

Fleetwood, Nicole. 2004. "'Busing It' in the City: Black Youth, Performance, and Public Transit." *Drama Review* 48 (2): 33–48. http://dx.doi.org/10.1162/105420404323063382

Goldstein, Daniel. 2010. *The Spectacular City: Violence and Performance in Urban Bolivia*. Durham, NC: Duke University Press.

Gordon, Avery. 1997. *Ghostly Matters: Haunting and the Sociological Imagination*. Minneapolis: University of Minnesota Press.

Guano, Emanuela. 2002. "Ruining the President's Spectacle: Theatricality and Telepolitics in the Buenos Aires Public Sphere." *Journal of Visual Culture* 1 (3): 303–23. http://dx.doi.org/10.1177/147041290200100304

Guano, Emanuela. 2003. "A Stroll through La Boca: The Politics and Poetics of Spatial Experience in a Buenos Aires Neighborhood." *Space and Culture* 6 (4): 356–76. http://dx.doi.org/10.1177/1206331203257250

Guano, Emanuela. 2007. "Respectable Ladies and Uncouth Men: The Performative Politics of Class and Gender in the Public Realm of an Italian City." *Journal of American Folklore* 120 (475): 48–72. http://dx.doi.org/10.1353/jaf.2007.0011

Harms, Erik. 2010. *Saigon's Edge*. Minneapolis: University of Minnesota Press.

Holston, James, and Arjun Appadurai. 1999. "Cities and Citizenship." In *Cities and Citizenship*, ed. James Holston, 1–16. Durham, NC: Duke University Press.

Ingold, Tim, and Jo L. Vergunst, eds. 2008. *Ways of Walking: Ethnography and Practice on Foot*. Aldershot, UK: Ashgate.

Irving, Andrew. 2010. "Dangerous Substances and Visible Evidence: Tears, Blood, Alcohol, Pills." *Visual Studies* 25 (1): 24–35. http://dx.doi.org/10.1080/14725861003606753

Irving, Andrew. 2015. "New York Stories." *Ethnos: Journal of Anthropology* 81: 1–21.

Juris, Jeffrey, and Maple Razsa. 2011. "Occupy, Anthropology, and the 2011 Global Uprisings." *Cultural Anthropology Online*, "Fieldsights: Hot Spots." http://culanth.org/fieldsights/63-occupy-anthropology-and-the-2011-global-uprisings

Legat, Allice. 2008. "Walking Stories, Leaving Footprints." In *Ways of Walking: Ethnography and Practice on Foot*, eds. Tim Ingold and Jo L. Vergunst, 35–47. Aldershot, UK: Ashgate.

Low, Setha, and Neil Smith, eds. 2006. *The Politics of Public Space*. New York: Routledge.

Lund, Katrin. 2008. "Listen to the Sound of Time: Walking with Saints in an Andalusian Village." In *Ways of Walking: Ethnography and Practice on Foot*, eds. Tim Ingold and Jo L. Vergunst, 93–103. Aldershot, UK: Ashgate.

Lyon-Callo, Vincent. 2008. *Inequality, Poverty, and Neoliberal Governance: Activist Ethnography in the Homeless Sheltering Industry*. Toronto: University of Toronto Press.

Malkki, Liisa. 2007. "Tradition and Improvisation in Ethnographic Field Research." In *Improvising Theory: Process and Temporality in Ethnographic Fieldwork*, eds. Allaine Cerwonka and Liisa Malkki, 163–86. Chicago: University of Chicago Press.

Mitchell, Don. 1995. "The End of Public Space? People's Park, Definitions of the Public, and Democracy." *Annals of the Association of American Geographers* 85 (1): 108–33.

Moretti, Cristina. 2011. "The Wandering Ethnographer: Researching and Representing the City through Everyday Encounters." *Anthropologica*. Special Theme Issue: New Directions in Experimental and Engaged Ethnography 53 (2): 245–55.

Moretti, Cristina. 2015. *Milanese Encounters: Public Space and Vision in Contemporary Italy*. Toronto: University of Toronto Press.

Navaro-Yashin, Yael. 2009. "Affective Spaces, Melancholic Objects: Ruination and the Production of Anthropological Knowledge." *Journal of the Royal Anthropological Institute* 15 (1): 1–18. http://dx.doi.org/10.1111/j.1467-9655.2008.01527.x

O'Neill, Maggie, and Phil Hubbard. 2010. "Walking, Sensing, Belonging: Ethno-mimesis as Performative Praxis." *Visual Studies* 25 (1): 46–58. http://dx.doi.org/10.1080/14725861003606878

Partridge, Damani. 2008. "We Were Dancing in the Club, Not on the Berlin Wall: Black Bodies, Street Bureaucrats, and Exclusionary Incorporation into the New Europe." *Cultural Anthropology* 23 (4): 660–87. http://dx.doi.org/10.1111/j.1548-1360.2008.00022.x

Pink, Sarah. 2008. "An Urban Tour: The Sensory Sociality of Ethnographic Place-Making." *Ethnography* 9 (2): 175–96. http://dx.doi.org/10.1177/1466138108089467

Pink, Sarah, Phil Hubbard, Maggie O'Neill, and Alan Radley. 2010. "Walking across Disciplines: From Ethnography to Arts Practice." *Visual Studies* 25 (1): 1–7. http://dx.doi.org/10.1080/14725861003606670

Pratt, Minnie Bruce. 1988. "Identity: Skin, Blood, Heart." In *Yours in Struggle: Three Feminist Perspectives on Anti-Semitism and Racism*, eds. Elly Bulkin, Minnie Bruce Pratt, and Barbara Smith, 11–63. Ithaca, NY: Firebrand Books.

Razack, Sherene. 2000. "Gendered Racial Violence and Spatialized Justice: The Murder of Pamela George." *Canadian Journal of Law and Society* 15 (2): 91–130. http://dx.doi.org/10.1017/S0829320100006384

Rosenblum, Ely. 2013. "If One Night." Centre for Imaginative Ethnography. http://imaginativeethnography.org/galleria/if-one-night-an-ethnographic-soundscape-and-commentaries

Schielke, Samuli. 2012. "Surfaces of Longing: Cosmopolitan Aspiration and Frustration in Egypt." *City & Society* 24 (1): 29–37. http://dx.doi.org/10.1111/j.1548-744X.2012.01066.x

Schielke, Samuli. 2013. "Engaging the World on the Alexandria Waterfront." In *The Global Horizon: Expectations of Migration in Africa and the Middle East*, eds. Knut Graw and Samuli Schielke, 175–92. Leuven, Belgium: Leuven University Press.

Tonnelat, Stephane. 2008. "Out of Frame: The Invisible Life of Urban Interstices—a Case Study in Carenton-le-Pont, Paris, France." *Ethnography* 9 (3): 291–324. http://dx.doi.org/10.1177/1466138108094973

Truitt, Allison. 2008. "On the Back of a Motorbike: Middle-Class Mobility in Ho Chi Minh City, Vietnam." *American Ethnologist* 35 (1): 3–19. http://dx.doi.org/10.1111/j.1548-1425.2008.00002.x

Tsing, Anna Lowenhaupt. 1993. *In the Realm of the Diamond Queen*. Princeton, NJ: Princeton University Press.

Tsing, Anna Lowenhaupt. 2005. *Friction: An Ethnography of Global Connections*. Princeton, NJ: Princeton University Press.

Tuck-Po, Lye. 2008. "Before a Step Too Far: Walking with Batek Hunter-Gatherers in the Forests of Pahang, Malaysia." In *Ways of Walking: Ethnography and Practice on Foot*, eds. Tim Ingold and Jo L. Vergunst, 21–34. Aldershot, UK: Ashgate.

Vigh, Henrik. 2009. "Motion Squared: A Second Look at the Concept of Social Navigation." *Anthropological Theory* 9 (4): 419–38. http://dx.doi.org/10.1177/1463499609356044

Walsh, Andrew. 2012. *Made in Madagascar: Sapphires, Ecotourism, and the Global Bazaar*. Toronto: University of Toronto Press.

Wyman, Julie. 2009. "Acting (on) Our Own Discomforts: BLW's [Media] Performance as Research." In *Mapping Landscapes for Performance as Research: Scholarly Acts and Creative Cartographies*, eds. Lynette Hunter and Shannon Rose Riley, 223–29. Basingstoke, UK: Palgrave Macmillan.

Notes

1   See a photo of Iacchetti's bench at www.giulioiacchetti.com/?p=785

2   See a video of Brunsing's bench at www.fabianbrunsing.de

3   See a video of Esterni's bench at www.esterni.it

4　During the Stories and Plays Project that Culhane "co-created" with residents of Vancouver's Downtown Eastside and graduate students, participants shared, constructed, and performed stories together (Culhane 2011, 258). The people involved in the project first agreed to participate in the first series of workshops. They signed the second consent forms to continue the meetings and to be part of a final performance that they decided collaboratively. Lastly, the participants were asked if they agreed to the project being represented and discussed through publications, and were given the option that no academic products be generated from the project. As Culhane explains, obtaining informed consent in several stages, and understanding it as a developing relationship rather than a one-time contract, recognizes the "performative principle" of ethnography: "that meaning emerges in the performance of storytelling and reception by diverse audiences" and that as a consequence, consent should be negotiated not just before but also during and after the performance (2011, 261). The goal of this method in the Stories and Plays Project was to experiment with alternative "ethical engagements" between ethnographers and participants, and to counter exploitative practices in research in a marginalized neighborhood where residents are routinely "mined for data" (Culhane 2011, 261). This approach, moreover, helps shift the focus of attention from the end products to the process of ethnography and the kinds of relations, insights, and experiences it creates (Culhane 2011, 261; see also Centre for Imaginative Ethnography at www.imaginativeethnography.org).

5　See an interview with Irving at http://blog.wennergren.org/2013/06/interview-dr-andrew-irving-new-york-stories

6　I thank Erin Martineau for her insightful suggestions on this point.

7　See Websites under Additional Resources for more information about this project.

8　See Websites under Additional Resources for more information about this project.

CHAPTER 6

PERFORMING

Magdalena Kazubowski-Houston

IMAGE 6.1: Ethnographic performance *Horses and Angels*.
The performance was developed in collaboration with Polish student actors
in 2003 and explored unequal gender relations in Poland.

Credit: Foto Bannach Elbląg.

I almost wish I hadn't gone down the rabbit-hole—and yet—and yet—
it's rather curious, you know, this sort of life! I do wonder what can have
happened to me! When I used to read fairy tales, I fancied that kind of
thing never happened, and now here I am in the middle of one!
    —Lewis Carroll, Alice's Adventures in Wonderland (1993, 61)

Randia—an elderly Polish Roma woman and my long-time interlocutor[1]—
once remarked, "You must write a fairy tale about us—because when you

come here, it's like a fairy tale, like magic, and when you leave, it's all gone—
we could then perform it like a play, like we did before" (field notes 2012).
Randia's request hit me like a rush of air, as though Alice's White Rabbit had
just run past me, his watch in his waistcoat pocket. For over a decade, I have
worked with Roma minorities in Elbląg, Poland, studying their everyday
encounters with prejudice, discrimination, and violence. During this time,
I have been committed to exploring the intersections of ethnography and
imagination, using theater and performance as both ethnographic processes and
products. I practice what can be referred to as "performance of ethnography"
(performance as ethnographic representation) and "performance as ethnography" (performance as ethnographic process). Performance and ethnography
can be combined in various ways. One can conduct research and then develop
a performance based on it; use a performance development process as a way
of conducting fieldwork; or use performance as an ethnographic process that
culminates in a publicly staged performance.

In an earlier project, I approached my research by employing theater
as a means of participant observation and representation. In collaboration
with a group of Roma women and local actors from Elbląg, I developed a
theater performance through rehearsals to learn about Roma women's experiences of violence. The performance was staged in a local cultural center for
Roma and non-Roma audiences. Subsequently, I analyzed the power relations that defined our mutual interactions within the ethnographic process
itself (Kazubowski-Houston 2010). In another project, I adopted dramatic
storytelling as an ethnographic method to study the impact of transnational
migration on Roma women's experiences of aging.

Although Randia and I worked together on both projects, I was a bit
dumbfounded by her request that I write a fairy tale. I had dramatized excerpts
from my field notes, but primarily I worked collaboratively with my interlocutors as storytellers, playwrights, directors, actors, and designers. While they
had used fictional accounts to stage their life stories, I had never written an
entirely fictional script myself, never mind an ethnographic fairy tale. While
I had trained professionally as a theater director, my relationship with Randia
could not be easily imagined apart from our roles as anthropologist and interlocutor. But how does one write an ethnographic fairy tale—one that could
be staged? What would it be about? Who would our audience be? As my
questions multiplied, my excitement grew. There was something enticing in
Randia's request—a promising rabbit hole, a new journey into imagination.

I approach imagination not as an abstract faculty, but rather—like other
contributors to this book—as diverse and "messy" imaginative practices and
creative methodologies (see "Imagining: An Introduction" for more discussion
on these terms). "Imaginative practices" are the social practices constituted by

human/nonhuman relations, and the historical, social, and cultural contexts in which they are embedded; "creative methodologies" are the transdisciplinary, collaborative, embodied, and critical approaches to research that bridge ethnography, anthropology, and the arts. In embarking upon the fairy tale project, I would attend to the imaginative practices that constitute my fieldwork relations, Randia's life circumstances, and her relationship to me as an anthropologist. As a creative methodology, this project would bring fiction, performance, and ethnography into conversation, in a critical, reflexive, and collaborative ethnographic inquiry.

Imaginative practices are frequently incidental, unintended, and improvisational—and generative. I am inspired by Vincent Crapanzano's (2004, 19) observation that imagination allows us "to project our 'fables' in a direction that does not have to reckon with the 'evident universe.'" Breaking with the evident, the expected, can conjure up new ways of being, dreams, and desires, shifting our focus toward what surfaces, sprouts, and promises (Mittermaier 2011, 30; Crapanzano 2004, 14–15). This generative capacity, however, cannot be understood solely in utopian terms; as "an impulse of real life" (Ingold 2013, 735), imagination can both empower and disempower, subvert oppression and sustain it. Imagination can imbue us with happiness, hope, and strength, just as much as it can fill us with sadness, despair, and resignation.

In embarking on the fairy tale project, it was this anticipatory, creative, and uncertain potential—not really knowing where I was headed—that I found exhilarating, if also anxiety provoking. So: like Alice, down the rabbit hole I went. Down, down, down . . . until, suddenly, I landed with a thump. I jumped to my feet and looked around. Nothing in sight but a big filing cabinet standing in front of me. I peered inside . . . and there it was: a stash of my field notes, diaries, and interview transcripts. I thumbed through them, feeling like I was still falling. How to turn this heap of papers into a fairy tale? Almost ready to throw in the towel, I realized that I needed to sketch out for myself the differences between an "ethnographic" and a "regular" work of fiction. I wouldn't want to confuse the Mouse's "tale" with its "tail," like Alice did.

Boundaries

Since the 1980s "crisis of representation" (Clifford and Marcus 1986)—a skepticism about ethnography as an adequate means to describe social reality—most anthropologists have come to see ethnographic truths as partial and subjective (Behar 1996, 2007; Abu-Lughod 1993; Geertz 1988; Clifford and Marcus 1986). Debating the differences between ethnographic monographs and literary fiction, some saw them as two sides of the same coin: a Tweedledum and Tweedledee of sorts, garrulous twins constantly bickering to assert their identities, yet unable to part. If ethnographic knowledge is partial and subjective, how is it different from a work of fiction? While the border between ethnography and fiction may not be easy to discern, most anthropologists would agree that ethnography is rooted in fieldwork and accountable to the people it represents (Narayan 1999, 42; Clifford and Marcus 1986), while fiction invents the world at will (Narayan 1999, 135). Didier Fassin (2014, 41) writes that while a novelist conjures up a world, an anthropologist seeks to convey the real (what has happened) and to articulate the true (what ought to be brought to light) (see Denielle Elliott's chapter, "Writing," in this volume).

Such debates have sparked much experimentation, with anthropologists trying their hand at different literary genres, seeking a more evocative, embodied, and accessible means of expression than the traditional, specialist, ethnographic monograph. Anthropologists have incorporated literary conventions (such as suspense and exaggeration) (Ashforth 2000); improvised upon interlocutors' stories (Myerhoff 1980); made anonymous research locales and characters (Elliott 2014; Kazubowski-Houston 2012); invented locales, characters, or events, as inspired by one's fieldwork (Augé 2013); and shifted between ethnographic accuracy and fictional invention (Stewart 1989). Despite this blurring of genres, however, few anthropologists have been willing to do away with boundaries entirely. Tweedledum and Tweedledee were similar— but not identical, after all!

Having considered the differences between ethnography and fiction, I decided to write a fictional dramatic script based on my fieldwork and relationships with my Roma interlocutors, in the form of a fairy tale. But I had no idea how to even begin. My enthusiasm withered like a violet in a drought, and Alice's "DRINK ME" bottle was nowhere in sight. It occurred to me that perhaps I needed to learn more about fairy tales to be able to write one.

The Fairy Tale Genre

The fairy tale—usually based on oral folk tales (Foster 2012, 8; Zipes 2012, 11)— is a literary genre of fiction that incorporates fantastical characters, events, and locales, and serves both entertaining and didactic functions (Sikharulidze 2012, 91). Fairy tales often comment on how people face and respond to life-changing events or problems (Zipes 2012, xi). Generally, a theatrical adaption of a fairy tale transforms the tale's narrative into dramatic action and its characters into dramatis personae (Spangler 2013, 16). Anthropologists and folklorists have analyzed fairy tales in terms of their social meanings and functions, using semiotic, hermeneutic, structural, comparative, and psychoanalytic perspectives (see, for example, Zipes, 2012; Shokeid 1982; Propp [1928] 1968; Levi-Strauss 1955, 1979). Feminist and critical race studies scholars and activists have critiqued fairy tales for perpetuating normative gender ideals that maintain dominant systems of power (Zipes 2012), and for their racialized stereotypes of subaltern people (Stewart 2000). Others have reworked popular fairy tales to destabilize patriarchal discourses (Williams 2012) and to create a space in which women may imagine alternative realities (Severin 2003).

While I decided to take on this fairy tale project primarily because Randia had asked me to, I also thought that it might be beneficial to explore the genre as a mode of ethnographic inquiry and reflection. I suspected that its fictional and fantastical characteristics, which encourage the imagination and open a window onto a character's thoughts and emotions, could potentially carve inroads into "imaginative lifeworlds" (Irving 2011, 22)—interior dialogues, thoughts, moods, and feelings—that cannot always be easily accessed through conventional ethnographic methods but are an important part of lived experience. I hoped that such insights would afford me a different kind of understanding of my interlocutors' circumstances and our relationships that perhaps would be more attuned to the affective and embodied dimensions of our lives and, consequently, facilitate a more critical and reflexive construction of ethnographic knowledge. I also thought that the fictional anonymity of the fairy tale would potentially allow me to reflect upon the more private aspects of my relationship with Randia too confidential to explore publicly, especially if Randia ultimately decided to have the tale performed in front of an audience.

Writing a Fairy Tale

I began to have some ideas about how to approach my writing. First, I needed to think about how the fairy tale could easily be adapted for the stage. Trained as a theater director, I knew there were many options. I was Alice, again, looking down a corridor with many doors! I could write an ethnographic fairy tale in prose form and then adapt it for the stage, or I could write a play or a dramatic scenario (often used in nontraditional, "devised,"[2] or "physical"[3] theater) as a blueprint from which to create a performance. A dramatic scenario—written in either descriptive or poetic form—specifies the locale, dramatis personae, and outline of dramatic action. Had Randia not specifically requested that I write the fairy tale myself, I could have developed a script in rehearsals in collaboration with actors through improvisation.[4] In the end, I decided to write the fairy tale in poetic prose; I would first fictionalize the characters, locales, and events, and then adapt it for the stage.

Inspired by feminist and other critiques of fairy tales, I thought that my tale could speak about Randia's (and other Roma women's) courage and perseverance in the face of oppression and poverty. I would try to say something about how recent transnational migration had transformed experiences of aging. In Poland, the quality of life has deteriorated for Roma since the fall of state socialism. Negative stereotypes, combined with economic crises and Polish nationalist sentiments, have increased the stigmatization of, and violence against, this minority group. As a result, many younger and middle-aged Roma have migrated to Western Europe and the United Kingdom, leaving behind many elderly who are unable to travel due to ill health or age. My fairy tale could tell the story of how Randia has coped—in the absence of her younger relatives—in this context. I wanted the characters, locales, events, and images to stand as metaphors for the relentless hardships Randia faces, her determination to live what she believes to be a good life, the loneliness she frequently conveys when talking about her blindness and her far-away children, her courage in continuing to tell fortunes, and her generosity in supporting her children and grandchildren, both morally and financially, against all odds.

Someone once told me that fairy tales are about "undoing yourself into the world." Perhaps a first step in this direction would be to approach my fairy tale as an exercise in anthropological reflexivity: I could reflect upon the impact of my presence in my interlocutors' lives. I could have the characters and their actions represent my long, complicated relationship with Randia. I have known Randia for 15 years, and she has been one of my most important teachers and a close confidante; however, in recent years, her isolation and her deteriorating sight had transformed our relationship into one of interdependence. She had grown more reliant on my help with performing daily tasks, and I had started feeling a greater responsibility for her well-being. I thought this would be an important aspect of my research to communicate through my fairy tale.

When I first sat down to write, the image of a hump flashed into my head. More precisely, the hump of a hunchback. What did it mean? I wasn't sure— but how remarkable! Maybe it was a creative spark, one that "at the right moment will burst into flame" (Taussig 2011, 118). Lisa Stevenson (2014, 10) argues that images are good to think with because they force us to inhabit uncertainty, which is often avoided in ethnography. I let myself think with the hump. An image, a spark, an open door . . . "Iridescence" is what I found.

Iridescence

A long, long time ago, and far, far away, behind one big mountain and behind another big mountain, there lived Very Tall Old Woman. She lived in a village in a quite tall hut with her quite tall children and her quite tall grandchildren. The other villagers were very small, so small in fact that they never bothered to look Very Tall Old Woman directly in the eye. And Very Tall Old Woman was tall, so tall in fact that she could not look them directly in the eye, either. Very Tall Old Woman worked very hard at putting food on the family table and coal in the family hearth. Late every night, she would quietly crawl out of bed, don her nightgown, and venture out into the mountains. She would climb up one big mountain and then climb up another big mountain, and because she was so very tall, she would sweep past this star and past that star, gathering up their pearls of iridescence with her mighty eyes. Light would surge through her body and fill her up with such formidable warmth that with each surge she would grow a few inches taller, and her hair would gray a few strands grayer. In time, she would lower her head down, cup her palms to her eyes, and wait . . . and wait . . . until a stream of stardust would cascade from her eyes into her palms. And so every night, Very Tall Old Woman would return home with her gown pockets brimming with stardust. The following day, on each and every day, as the sun crested the mountain peaks, she would go to the village square and sell sachets of stardust to the villagers for a few copper coins, a few portions of bread, a bunch of carrots, a handful of potatoes, or a basket of strawberries. One day, however, while selling sachets of stardust in the old village square, Very Old Tall Woman chanced upon Very Short Young Girl, who looked Very Tall Old Woman directly in the eye; and Very Tall Old Woman looked Very Short Young Girl directly in the eye too. And from that day on, Girl began visiting Woman in her hut, learning her ways of life, helping her with chores and errands, and the two became dear friends.

The friendship between Woman and Girl continued for years and years, until the day of the great earthquake, when the villagers, including Woman's children and grandchildren, were swallowed up whole. Woman and Girl were the only ones spared. Yet Woman did not escape the earthquake unscathed. Tectonic shards shot up from the ground and took the sight from her eyes. Now blind, her life changed forever. No more climbing over one big mountain and over another big mountain. No more sweeping past the stars' iridescence. No more gathering stardust. No more surges of warmth through her body. She spent most of her days sitting alone in her hut with her vacant eyes turned skyward. But then, one day, she developed an intense itch in the gulley of her back. She scratched and scratched her itch, but the more she scratched, the more it itched. And soon the itch bloomed into a bump, and that bump bloomed into a hump, so big in fact that she could barely move. It kept blooming and blooming until it broke through the roof of her hut. And it was then that she felt a strange tingling on her hump, and asked Girl to come take a look. Posthaste she came, examined the hump, and told Woman of a tiny door at the tingly spot. Curious, Woman asked Girl to open it. A wave of familiar warmth rushed out through the door and enveloped Woman, who grew a few inches taller and grayed a few strands grayer. Mesmerized, she asked Girl to enter through the door. Girl was gone one long minute, and then another long minute, and after several long minutes, returned and told Woman how the hump was filled with iridescence and warmth. And that off in the distance she could see two mountains shimmering like gold. Woman asked the Girl to climb up the one big mountain and climb up the other big mountain, and to sweep past the stars and then return back. So Girl was gone for one long hour and another long hour while Woman waited eagerly. But to her dismay, Girl returned to report that she was too short to sweep past the stars. Woman instructed her to try once again. So Girl went back to the top of one mountain and the top of another mountain, and stretched up on the tips of her toes, but again could not reach the stars. In grief she looked up at the stars, and let forth such a terrible cry that the hump of Woman trembled and quaked. And from the firmament fell fast iridescence into Girl's upturned eyes. The light surged through her body, and filled her up with such formidable warmth that with each surge Girl grew a few inches taller, and her hair grayed a few strands grayer. But Woman kept trembling and quaking, and Girl kept growing and graying. When all was finally quiet, Girl lowered her head down, cupped her palms to her eyes, and a stream of stardust cascaded from her eyes into her palms. She returned to the door with her pockets brimming with stardust, but Girl had grown so tall, that she could no longer walk through the door, and Girl had grown so old that she could no longer crawl through it. So she scooped the stardust out from one pocket, and out from another pocket, and passed it through to Woman. But as the stardust crossed the threshold, the inside of the hump went dark and cold. And as soon as it touched Woman's hands, it coated them with hoarfrost, which surged through her body, and filled her up with such formidable cold that with each surge Woman shrank a few inches smaller . . . and smaller . . . until she was finally gone.

Ethnographic Experimentation

It was time to plunge into adapting the fairy tale for the stage. This is always the most exciting, albeit capricious, part of the process for me. I feel like I'm at Alice's "mad tea party," with the March Hare, the Hatter, and the somnolent Dormouse, attempting to solve riddle after riddle.

In the last few decades, anthropology and cognate fields have taken up performance as an approach to research and representation. This has been largely a response to post-modern critiques of scientific positivism and the power imbalances in research relationships, and it has spawned a wide range of ethnographic experiments. Anthropologists and researchers across the disciplines have used a variety of terms—"performance ethnography," "performative ethnography," "ethnographic theatre," and "ethnodrama," to name a few—in reference to these experiments.

My fairy tale project used performance as a form of ethnographic representation, and, as such, can be best understood as a performance of ethnography. In fact, most performance-centered ethnography has been conducted at the level of representation, dating back to the early-1980s collaborations between anthropologists Victor Turner and Edith Turner and performance studies scholar/theater director Richard Schechner. These took place at a time when the anthropological focus had begun shifting from function to process and from structure to performance. The Turners and Schechner used performance as "instructional theatre" to represent fieldwork data to facilitate a "kinetic" learning process about another culture's way of life (Schechner 1985; Turner and Turner 1982). The Turners and Schechner involved students in staging pieces of existing ethnographic writing on ritual (e.g., on puberty rites and marriage ceremonies) to give them a more embodied understanding, rather than the descriptive and detached representations found in ethnographic monographs (Turner and Turner 1982, 33–34).

The crisis of representation, blurred genres, and performative turns that beset anthropology and other disciplines engendered epistemological[5] and ethical[6] questions about empirical research. Researchers across the disciplines began to examine performance's potential for communication and pedagogy (see, for example, Denzin 2003; Saldaña 2003; Mienczakowski 1995, 2000). Health researcher Jim Mienczakowski, for example, creates scripts based on fieldwork conducted in health care settings. He refers to these critical "ethnodramas" (Mienczakowski 1995, 360) as "acceptable fictions"—created by the ethnographer based on informant interviews but vetted by informants for accuracy (Mienczakowski 2000, 136). The scripts are circulated within health care communities for feedback and subsequently performed by medical or nursing students for various health stakeholders. Similarly, Norman Denzin (2003) creates performative ethnographic scripts to be read aloud, which bridge autoethnography,[7] performance, and commentary. Some scholars have criticized a performance of ethnography approach, arguing that it assumes that the "truth" about another culture is more authentically represented and expressed through theater than through writing. This was the primary reason why I had, thus far, refrained from developing a theater performance based on ethnographic material without the collaboration of my interlocutors. Now, however, the fairy tale project demanded that I give it a try. What I needed to do, though, was to tailor it in ways that would mesh with what I believe about anthropology and ethnography. My intent was not to create a "more authentic" ethnographic product, but rather to transform this making of a performative fairy tale into an ethnographic process itself.

Experiments with ethnographic process—performance as ethnography—have been relatively rare. In anthropology, Johannes Fabian (1990) has been a trailblazer. Working with a theater troupe in Shaba, Zaire, he employed theater performance as a form of participant observation, addressing his research questions by collaboratively developing a theater performance with his interlocutors. Fabian (19) advanced a "performative"—as opposed to "informative"—ethnography, in which the ethnographer becomes a co-performer who does research "*with*, not *of*" the people with whom he works (43). Other explorations include Dwight Conquergood's (1988) ethnography as street performance in a Hmong refugee camp in Thailand; Soyini Madison's (2010) use of performance as a form of activism and human rights intervention in Ghana; my own work with Polish Roma, using performance as participant observation in the study of power within my ethnographic process (Kazubowski-Houston 2010); Dara Culhane's (2011) utopian improvisational ethnography conducted in collaboration with residents of Vancouver's Downtown Eastside; the work by Lee Papa and Luke Eric Lassiter (2003) on ethnography as performative and collaborative community engagement; and Virginie Magnat's (2012) performance as a collaborative and ethnographic "ceremony" honoring Indigenous ways of knowing.

Rather than dramatizing my field notes and interview transcripts, I would engage in improvisational writing, allowing ideas to freely spill onto the page and characters to spontaneously emerge. An ethnography of chance (see Taussig 2011, 59–60, where he talks about "chance in fieldwork"), an ethnography of surprise! What "imaginative horizons" would open up (Crapanzano 2004)? What ethnographic "truths" would be constructed through this process?

Theater and performance studies scholars have long held that improvisation—where content is created in the moment—can lead to discovery and unintended outcomes (Peters 2009). Michael Taussig (2011, 19) writes that "words written down in feverish haste score a bull's eye." Certainly, not every improvisation will hit the mark—the vulnerability of improvisation can at times hinder creativity, leading one to fall back on familiar clichés. I felt, however, that even such moments of "falling back" could provide me with novel insights into my relationship with Randia. As well, improvisation made sense to me theatrically; as a theater director, it frequently helped me to generate more compelling dramatic material. Qualitative researcher and theater practitioner Johnny Saldaña (2003, 220) reminds us that performance ethnographers should strive to create engaging, sophisticated, and affective ethnographic representations. Who wants to listen to the Dormouse drone on and on?

For Saldaña (2003, 220), the primary goal of theater is to explore ideas and to entertain the audience. Others argue that performance-centered research should educate and provoke (see, for example, Kazubowski-Houston 2010, 2011; Madison 2005; Denzin 2003; Conquergood 1988, 1991). This argument draws on Bertolt Brecht's (1964) notion of the politicization of theater; Brecht, a theater theoretician, playwright, and director, asserted that theater should engage audience members in questioning and challenging the status quo. I wanted the fairy tale to invite the audience to think critically about the issues represented without rendering it a soapbox for our ideas. I thus balanced an improvisational mode of writing with sketching out in advance some of the issues with which I wanted the audience to engage critically.

Imagining Performance

The next step in adapting the fairy tale for the stage was to decide where, for whom, and how I would stage it. To me, this phase is about negotiating the ethnographic aspects with the "aesthetic expressive" (Edwards 1997). This is

IMAGE 6.2: Randia.

Credit: Magdalena Kazubowski-Houston, 2013.

an imaginative and challenging practice of figuring out how to tell our field stories, not descriptively, but through visual and embodied metaphors. There are a variety of ways that one could approach staging: I could first develop the performance on my own with a group of actors and then ask Randia to provide feedback. This type of approach is useful when our interlocutors are not willing or able to participate personally in rehearsals; given Randia's recent health challenges, this approach seemed a good option. Alternatively, I could work on the project with graduate students and stage it for the community, or I could hire actors in Elbląg and stage it in a local community center for Roma and non-Roma audiences.

Then I began to flesh out the artistic aspects of the performance. I immediately saw that it could take the form of physical theater, although any mode of performance would be suitable for this project, including realist theater,[8] street theater,[9] puppetry,[10] clowning,[11] and more. For me, trained in physical theater, this mode was an obvious choice, which would privilege an experiential and embodied epistemology. Recognizing the importance of this form, Conquergood (1991, 189) asserts that the foundation of a performance does not always lie in the spoken text, because ideas and emotions are also expressed in gestures, movements, sound, ritual action, and symbols. Similarly, Paul Stoller (1997, 23) calls for a "sensuous scholarship" that would "allow ethnographic things to capture us through our bodies [and senses]" (see Dara Culhane's chapter, "Sensing," in this volume).

In recent years, theories of affect have opened up new doors to thinking about how performance-centered ethnography could contribute to anthropological research. Such theories construe the notion of affect as the body's capacity to both affect and be affected and, consequently, its potential as a site of politics, activism, and alliance (Clough and Halley 2007; Ahmed 2004). I wanted my fairy tale performance to explore these theories in practice.

The mise-en-scène[12] of my physical theater piece would include three main characters: Very Tall Old Woman, Very Short Young Girl, and Narrator. The Narrator could relate the fairy tale's narrative, recite excerpts from my field notes and interviews, and explain to the audience which parts of the performance were fictional and which were ethnographic. I envisioned a small theater with rusted doors squeaking like bullfinches, an audience standing in a circle around a stage set up like a village square, and actors surrounded by the audience. Two mountains made of opalescent material—with the stage lights hitting the surface, suggesting peaks awash in sunlight—would rise upstage. In front of the mountains there would stand a tall, tattered, wooden hut with a large crooked door. Stage lights would dim and alternate between warmer (amber, yellow, orange) and colder (blue and white) hues. Perhaps the stage design and lighting would reflect the contrast between Randia's determined and generous spirit and the austerity of her life circumstances.

Very Tall Old Woman would wear a long, red dress with a black shawl, and be barefoot, while Very Short Young Girl would be clad in a black dress, red shawl, and red shoes. As such, the costumes would evoke the reciprocity that defined my relationship with Randia. A quiet soundtrack of minimalist music, perhaps by Philip Glass, could play in the background to underscore the relentlessness of Very Tall Old Woman's hardships. I could choreograph the performance with the actors during rehearsals through discussions and improvisations. We might begin by dividing the entire scenario into smaller scenes and identifying themes, moods, and central images. According to theater director and practitioner Augusto Boal, improvisation—bypassing the censorship of the rational brain—connects to subconscious feelings and desires (as described in Jackson 1992, xxiii). For me, improvisation allows me to treat a performance as an embodied and affective ethnographic research process, and not just a representation. I could also hold post-performance discussions to learn what audience members thought about the performance's content and the use of theater as a form of ethnography.

Collaboration

I could have, however, approached this ethnographic fairy tale project very differently. If Randia's health had been better and she had been able to participate in the project, we could have collaboratively written the fairy tale and co-developed the entire performance, making it a performance-as-ethnography project right from the start. Researchers working collaboratively are aware of the unequal power relations that define interactions between ethnographer and interlocutor, and they try to alter this dynamic so that interlocutors become participants in the research, directly involved in decision-making processes (Yeich 1996, 112–13).

If Randia had been able to be involved in the process, we could have co-written the fairy tale, together selecting which fieldwork stories to tell, and then deciding in what venue, for what audiences (Roma, non-Roma, local, Canadian, international), how (would we perform ourselves, or hire actors?), and in what style we would stage the performance. In rehearsals, we would have together created the physical and spoken texts; plot; character profiles; images; and stage, costume, sound, and lighting design. This might involve proposing ideas and negotiating a consensus, improvising scenes for one another or having actors do so, and then selecting material for inclusion.

Or, Randia could have taken the reins of the entire process, and I could have instead served as a facilitator, or as Fabian (1990, 7) aptly puts it, "a provider of occasions," who supplies the resources necessary to realize the project but exercises little control over the project's scope. Even such ethnographic processes are not, however, entirely equitable interactions, because no collaborative process is ever exempt from issues of power (Fabian 1990, 5). Power is implicated in both the production of knowledge and its applications in the real world, and conflicts can mar collaborative performance-centered research, just as they can any research project.

Stepping In

Now that I had written my fairy tale and imagined the project's next steps, we could begin rehearsals and explore these ideas in practice. Deeper into the rabbit hole we go. But perhaps there will be no rehearsals, perhaps this fairy tale will not be performed at all. Randia liked the fairy tale when I read it to her, and she hoped that one day we could stage it, but she remains too ill to take on a project of this scope. So this fairy tale might end up being a performance-centered ethnography without a performance—an unfinished journey into an unfinished world (Stewart 2008). Or rather, a performance of ethnographic imagination. What Taussig (2011, 22) so eloquently observed about fieldwork notebook drawing—that it "is important not for what it records so much as what it leads you on to see"—might also apply to performances of ethnographic imagination. Perhaps what they show is less important than where they take us—which rabbit holes they draw us into.

Writing the fairy tale and imagining the staging of it circuitously led me to the White Rabbit, Tweedledum and Tweedledee, the Mouse, and much more. The process has led me to a different way of doing ethnography. Attuned to the mystery of the image of a hump, I opened a door onto my unarticulated experiences, impressions, moods, and reveries (Irving 2011), and thus onto the unacknowledged fieldwork encounters that only reside somewhere deep within the rabbit holes of my unwritten "headnotes" (Ottenberg 1990, 144–48). "Iridescence," to which the White Rabbit brought me, attends to those aspects of Randia's life and my relationship with her that cannot be neatly packaged and explained away, but require "a way of listening . . . that . . . disrupts the security of what is known for sure" (Stevenson 2014, 2). Certain ideas broached by the fairy tale are, of course, precisely what I had originally set out to explore, including Randia's hardships, blindness, isolation, and loneliness; her resilient spirit and generosity; and our mutual dependence on each other. But other things emerged, too. And though they might be referred to as sadness, guilt, anger, dejection, helplessness, or hope, they cannot be easily pinned down. They "undo us into the world" like a skein of yarn, allowing us to grasp some of that magic that can only be found in fairy tales. And now, look!

Here he comes! The White Rabbit—do you feel the rush of air? See the watch in his waistcoat pocket, as he dives into the rabbit hole? Dare you follow?

Student Exercises

1. Write a short performance script based on your fieldwork experience: a dramatic dialogue between two characters; a dramatic scenario in a descriptive or poetic form outlining the main characters, locale, and dramatic action; or a fairy tale. Once you complete writing your short performance script, respond to the following questions: What aspects of your research were you trying to communicate through this exercise? What are the central metaphors and images in your piece, and how do they support its overall message? What are the challenges and potentials of representing ethnographic research through performative writing?

2. Write a one-page description explaining how you might adapt the ethnographic performance script you have written for the stage. Clearly outline the various aspects of stagecraft you would engage in, from planning, to rehearsing, to staging the performance. Discuss the performance's choreography and design (set, props, lighting, costumes). This does not have to be a conventional theater performance; instead, you could consider developing a street performance, performance art (an interdisciplinary blend of various art forms), clowning, puppetry, and the use of new media (such as image projections, a DJ mixing music live, smartphone/social media engagement, etc.). Once you complete the description, write a short paragraph about how you think the performance's dramatic text, the body, image, and sound may contribute to the construction and exchange of ethnographic knowledge.

Additional Resources

Websites

Centre for Imaginative Ethnography (CIE), Pedagogy/curricula
    http://imaginativeethnography.org/pedagogycurricula
Interdisciplined: Getting by with Anthropology and Improvised Theater
    http://bradfortier.com/2011/01/12/on-the-road-to-a-new-
    ethnography-anthropology-improvisation-and-performance
Cities@Manchester blog: New York Stories: The Lives of Other Citizens
    http://citiesmcr.wordpress.com/2011/12/12/new-york-stories-the-lives-
    of-other-citizens

Hemispheric Institute
http://hemisphericinstitute.org/hemi

Journals

Text & Performance Quarterly
www.tandfonline.com/loi/rtpq20?cookieSet=1
Qualitative Inquiry
http://qix.sagepub.com
TDR
www.mitpressjournals.org/loi/dram?cookieSet=1
Liminalities: A Journal of Performance Studies
http://liminalities.net

References

Abu-Lughod, Lila. 1993. *Writing Women's Worlds: Bedouin Stories*. Berkeley: University of California Press.

Ahmed, Sarah. 2004. *The Cultural Politics of Emotion*. New York: Routledge.

Ashforth, Adam. 2000. *Madumo: A Man Bewitched*. Chicago: University of Chicago: Press.

Augé, Marc. 2013. *No Fixed Abode*. Chicago: University of Chicago Press.

Behar, Ruth. 1996. *The Vulnerable Observer: Anthropology That Breaks Your Heart*. Boston: Beacon Press.

Behar, Ruth. 2007. "Ethnography in a Time of Blurred Genres." *Anthropology and Humanism* 32 (2): 145–55. http://dx.doi.org/10.1525/ahu.2007.32.2.145

Brecht, Bertolt. 1964. *Brecht on Theatre: The Development of an Aesthetic*. Trans. John Willett. New York: Hill and Wang.

Carroll, Lewis. 1993. *Alice's Adventures in Wonderland & Through the Looking-Glass*. Ware, UK: Wordsworth Editions.

Clifford, James, and George E. Marcus. 1986. *Writing Culture: The Poetics and Politics of Ethnography*. Berkeley: University of California Press.

Clough, Patricia Ticineto, and Jean Halley, eds. 2007. *The Affective Turn: Theorizing the Social*. Durham, NC: Duke University Press. http://dx.doi.org/10.1215/9780822389606

Conquergood, Dwight. 1988. "Health Theatre in a Hmong Refugee Camp: Performance, Communication, and Culture." *The Drama Review: A Journal of Performance Studies* 32(3): 174–208.

Conquergood, Dwight. 1991. "Rethinking Ethnography: Towards a Critical Cultural Politics." *Communication Monographs* 58 (2): 179–94. http://dx.doi.org/10.1080/03637759109376222

Crapanzano, Vincent. 2004. *Imaginative Horizons: An Essay in Literary-Philosophical Anthropology*. Chicago: University of Chicago Press.

Culhane, Dara. 2011. "Stories and Plays: Ethnography, Performance and Ethical Engagements." *Anthropologica* 53 (2): 229–43.

Denzin, Norman. 2003. *Performance Ethnography: Critical Pedagogy and the Politics of Culture*. Thousand Oaks, CA: Sage. http://dx.doi.org/10.4135/9781412985390

Edwards, Elizabeth. 1997. "Beyond the Boundary: A Consideration of the Expressive in Photography and Anthropology." In *Rethinking Visual Anthropology*, eds. Marcus Banks and Howard Morphy, 53–80. New Haven, CT: Yale University Press.

Elliott, Denielle. 2014. "Truth, Shame, Complicity, and Flirtation: An Unconventional, Ethnographic (Non)fiction." *Anthropology and Humanism* 39 (2): 145–58. http://dx.doi.org/10.1111/anhu.12052

Fabian, Johannes. 1990. *Power and Performance: Ethnographic Explorations through Proverbial Wisdom and Theatre in Shaba, Zaire*. Madison: University of Wisconsin Press.

Fassin, Didier. 2014. "True Life, Real Lives: Revisiting the Boundaries between Ethnography and Fiction." *American Ethnologist* 41 (1): 40–55. http://dx.doi.org/10.1111/amet.12059

Foster, Verna A. 2012. *Dramatic Revisions of Myths, Fairy Tales and Legends: Essays on Recent Plays*. Jefferson, NC: McFarland & Company.

Geertz, Clifford. 1988. *Works and Lives: An Anthropologist as Author*. Stanford, CA: Stanford University Press.

Ingold, Tim. 2013. "Dreaming of Dragons: On the Imagination of Real Life." *Journal of the Royal Anthropological Institute* 19 (4): 734–52. http://dx.doi.org/10.1111/1467-9655.12062

Irving, Andrew. 2011. "Strange Distance: Towards the Anthropology of Interior Dialogue." *Medical Anthropology Quarterly* 25 (1): 22–44. http://dx.doi.org/10.1111/j.1548-1387.2010.01133.x

Jackson, Adrian. 1992. "Translator's Introduction." In *Games for Actors and Non-Actors*, 1st ed., ed. Augusto Boal, xxii–xxvii. New York: Routledge.

Kazubowski-Houston, Magdalena. 2010. *Staging Strife: Lessons from Performing Ethnography with Polish Roma Women*. Montreal: McGill–Queen's University Press.

Kazubowski-Houston, Magdalena. 2011. "Thwarting Binarisms: Performing Racism in Postsocialist Poland." *Text and Performance Quarterly* 31 (2): 169–89. http://dx.doi.org/10.1080/10462937.2011.552118

Kazubowski-Houston, Magdalena. 2012. "A Stroll in Heavy Boots: Studying Polish Roma Women's Experiences of Ageing." *Canadian Theatre Review* 151: 16–23.

Levi-Strauss, Claude. 1955. "The Structural Study of Myth." *Journal of American Folklore* 68 (270): 428–44. http://dx.doi.org/10.2307/536768

Levi-Strauss, Claude. 1979. *The Origin of Table Manners: Introduction to a Science of Mythology*, vol. 3. New York: Harper & Row.

Madison, D. Soyini. 2005. *Critical Ethnography: Method, Ethics, and Performance*. Thousand Oaks, CA: Sage.

Madison, D. Soyini. 2010. *Acts of Activism: Human Rights as Radical Performance.* Cambridge: Cambridge University Press. http://dx.doi.org/10.1017/CBO9780511675973

Magnat, Virginie. 2012. "Can Research Become Ceremony? Performance Ethnography and Indigenous Epistemologies." *Canadian Theatre Review* 151: 30–6.

Mienczakowski, Jim. 1995. "The Theatre of Ethnography: The Reconstruction of Ethnography into Theatre with Emancipatory Potential." *Qualitative Inquiry* 1 (3): 360–75. http://dx.doi.org/10.1177/107780049500100306

Mienczakowski, Jim. 2000. "Ethnography in the Form of Theatre with Emancipatory Intentions." In *Research and Inequality*, eds. Carole Truman, Donna M. Merters, and Beth Humphries, 126–42. London: UCL Press.

Mittermaier, Amira. 2011. *Dreams That Matter: Egyptian Landscapes of the Imagination.* Berkeley: University of California Press.

Myerhoff, Barbara. 1980. *Number Our Days.* New York: Touchstone.

Narayan, Kirin. 1999. "Ethnography and Fiction: Where Is the Border?" *Anthropology and Humanism* 24 (2): 134–47. http://dx.doi.org/10.1525/ahu.1999.24.2.134

Ottenberg, Simon. 1990. "Thirty Years of Fieldnotes: Changing Relationships to the Text." In *Fieldnotes: The Making of Anthropology*, ed. Roger Sanjek, 139–60. Ithaca, NY: Cornell University Press.

Papa, Lee, and Luke Eric Lassiter. 2003. "The Muncie Race Riots of 1967: Representing Community Memory through Public Performance, and Collaborative Ethnography between Faculty, Students, and the Local Community." *Journal of Contemporary Ethnography* 32 (2): 147–66. http://dx.doi.org/10.1177/0891241602250883

Peters, Gary. 2009. *The Philosophy of Improvisation.* Chicago: University of Chicago Press. http://dx.doi.org/10.7208/chicago/9780226662800.001.0001

Propp, Vladimir. [1928] 1968. *Morphology of the Folktale.* Austin: University of Texas Press.

Saldaña, Johnny. 2003. "Dramatizing Data: A Primer." *Qualitative Inquiry* 9 (2): 218–36. http://dx.doi.org/10.1177/1077800402250932

Schechner, Richard. 1985. *Between Theatre and Anthropology.* Philadelphia: University of Pennsylvania Press.

Severin, Laura. 2003. "'The Gilt Is off the Gingerbread': Stevie Smith's Revisionary Fairy Tales." *Journal of Gender Studies* 12 (3): 203–14. http://dx.doi.org/10.1080/0958923032000141544

Shokeid, Moshe. 1982. "Toward an Anthropological Perspective of Fairy Tales." *Sociological Review* 30 (2): 223–33. http://dx.doi.org/10.1111/j.1467-954X.1982.tb00755.x

Sikharulidze, Ketevan. 2012. "Fairy-Tale as Genre." *Journal of Education* 1 (2): 91–94.

Spangler, Matthew. 2013. "Artist's Statement: Adapting T.C. Boyle's Novel *The Tortilla Curtain* and Subsequent Production by the San Diego Repertory Theatre." *Text and Performance Quarterly* 33 (2): 151–67. http://dx.doi.org/10.1080/10462937.2013.769061

Stevenson, Lisa. 2014. *Life beside Itself: Imagining Care in the Canadian Arctic.* Berkeley: University of California Press.

Stewart, John O. 1989. *Drinkers, Drummers, and Decent Folk: Ethnographic Narratives of Village Trinidad.* Albany, NY: SUNY Press.

Stewart, Kathleen. 2008. "Weak Theory in an Unfinished World." *Journal of Folklore Research* 45 (1): 71–82. http://dx.doi.org/10.2979/JFR.2008.45.1.71

Stewart, Michelle Pagni. 2000. "How Can This Be Cinderella If There Is No Glass Slipper? Native American 'Fairy Tales.'" *Studies in American Indian Literatures* 12 (1): 3–19.

Stoller, Paul. 1997. *Sensuous Scholarship.* Philadelphia: University of Pennsylvania Press. http://dx.doi.org/10.9783/9780812203134

Taussig, Michael. 2011. *I Swear I Saw This: Drawings in Fieldwork Notebooks, Namely My Own.* Chicago: University of Chicago Press. http://dx.doi.org/10.7208/chicago/9780226789842.001.0001

Turner, Victor, and Edith Turner. 1982. "Performing Ethnography." *The Drama Review: A Journal of Performance Studies* 26 (2): 33–50. http://dx.doi.org/10.2307/1145429

Williams, Christy. 2012. "Critical and Creative Perspectives on Fairy-Tales: An Intertextual Dialogue Between Fairy-Tale Scholarship and Postmodern Retellings (review)." *Marvels & Tales: Journal of Fairy-Tale Studies* 26 (2): 277–81.

Yeich, Susan. 1996. "Grassroots Organizing with Homeless People: A Participatory Research Approach." *Social Issues* 52 (1): 111–21. http://dx.doi.org/10.1111/j.1540-4560.1996.tb01364.x

Zipes, Jack. 2012. *The Irresistible Fairy Tale: The Social and Cultural History of a Genre.* Princeton, NJ: Princeton University Press.

Notes

1 Anthropologists employ different terms to refer to the people they work with, including "subjects," "informants," and "research participants," among others. I use the term "interlocutor" to indicate a person who takes an active role in a conversation, discussion, or dialogue (interlocution), in order to underscore the collaborative nature of my ethnographic research process.

2 The term "devised theater" usually refers to an original performance work developed collaboratively by a theater company or sometimes by an individual artist.

3 Physical theater is a performance that usually lacks a spoken text, and actors communicate primarily with gestures and movements.

4 Theatrical improvisation is a performance development process in which actors devise a performance's spoken and physical texts without a pre-existing script, either in rehearsals through games and exercises, or spontaneously in front of an audience.

5 Pertaining to questions of knowledge and knowledge acquisition.

6 Pertaining to questions of an anthropologist's professional responsibility and ethical conduct in ethnographic research.

7   Auto-ethnography is a reflexive style of anthropological writing that draws upon the anthropologist's own life story and experiences in the field, and reveals his or her research methodologies.

8   Realism in theater seeks to represent reality through "truthful" costumes, props (objects used by actors on stage), stage pieces, and make-up; the actor seeks to faithfully portray the character's thoughts and emotions.

9   Street theater is a type of performance that takes place in diverse public spaces (parks, parking lots, streets and sidewalks, shopping malls, etc.), and admission is generally free. It is frequently politically motivated and seeks to critique and subvert the status quo.

10 Puppetry is a form of performance wherein actors manipulate puppets and/or mannequins.

11 Clowning is a form of performance that employs slapstick, mime, or exaggerated gestures and movements, as well as juggling, humor, and comic situations.

12 "Mise-en-scène" is a French term that stands for all the elements of theatrical production: actors, scenery, lights, props, costumes, etc.

APPENDIX

RESOURCES FOR INSTRUCTORS

Chapter 2

All of the student exercises for this chapter could also be adopted in the classroom but here are a few more that might require additional instruction and guidance in the classroom setting.

1. Twitter Essay: What Is Ethnography?

After explaining and discussing the question "What is ethnography?" have the students answer the question in Twitter form. Ask them: Write a Twitter essay on #ethnography in 140 characters that examines or complicates the term. Don't waste a single character.

2. Collaborative Twitter Essay

Discuss Teju Cole's Twitter essay and collaborative writing strategies with students. Assign a topic, perhaps based on an ethnographic reading, and then have the students write a collaborative Twitter essay in class either using their Twitter accounts online or simply as a paper exercise. After, have students analyze the process and form, paying particular attention to collaborative writing strategies, tensions in co-writing, and co-construction of ideas.

3. Graphic Sketch

Discuss and explain the use of graphic novels in public anthropology, and have students read some examples (like those of Nick Sousanis or Lynda Barry). Get students to take notes during the class by only drawing images or pictures, to get them used to drawing. In the next class, consider giving them an ethnographic vignette that they must sketch out as a group. You can use Matt Madden's *99 Ways to Tell a Story* (2005) for more ideas and instruction on things like point of view, form, drawing techniques, and colors.

4. Stand-up Anthropology Comic Skit

I love the use of satire and humor in anthropology. It offers a medium to speak honestly, if subtly, about issues we often shy away from. In a classroom setting instructors might assign one or two short satirical readings (for instance, something by Kirsten Bell, Howard Campbell, or John Jackson, Jr.), have students view short video clips from comedians who touch on social issues related to the classroom (for instance, Russell Peters and ethnicity, or Sandra Shamas and perimenopause), or view Radi-Aid by SAIH in Norway, and then ask students to consider how they might use satire, parody, and humor in anthropology. Maybe daring students might like to do a stand-up anthropology comic skit for the class as an alternative to an oral presentation.

5. Field Notes: Written and Drawn

In projects where students are asked to do field notes, ask them to include both written and drawn descriptive notes.

6. Multimedia Final Projects

As an alternative to a final essay in senior-level undergraduate courses, consider assigning multimedia projects (collages, websites, skits, plays) or photo-essays so students are forced to learn new ways to translate their knowledge to audiences.

7. Instagram Mini-Essays

Instructors can combine students' love of Instagram with writing projects. You can create a course-specific hashtag (like #ANTH2016) and have students create micro-essays with an original photograph that they share on Instagram. This could be an interesting way to engage students across courses—from economic anthropology to sensorial ethnography. Another version of this could focus on a keyword in the spirit of Raymond Williams's *Keywords* (1985). Have students focus on describing or analyzing a concept from the photograph. For instance, a photograph of a Coca-Cola sign becomes a mini-essay explaining global capitalism. Instagram allows for a maximum of 2,200 characters, so this helps students learn concise writing skills.

8. Graphic Novel

Our contributor Alexadrine Bourdreault-Fournier has shared one of her class assignments that has students do graphic novels on the Centre for Imaginative Ethnography website. You can find it in the section on "Drawings."

Chapter 3

All the exercises offered in Chapter 3 are designed first for students and readers to carry out on their own as they work through the chapter. They are also designed for instructors to adapt for classroom exercises, and/or for homework exercises.

1. Sensescapes

"Sensescapes" are productive assignments. Students are asked to go for a walk in a designated area like the campus, their neighborhood, or their home and to create a "smellscape," and/or a "soundscape," and/or a "touchscape," and/or an "imagescape" by mapping the odors, sounds, objects, and sights they encounter. Analyze these in conversation with assigned readings and questions formulated by instructors.

2. Sensory Reading and Listening

Students are asked to record their sensory responses to reading an assigned text and listening to an assigned voice recording. How does piqued interest feel? Confusion? Frustration? Excitement? Empathy? Disgust? Fear? Amusement? How are these responses provoked? What associated ideas and memories are evoked? Analyze these in conversation with assigned readings and questions formulated by instructors.

3. Sensory Tasting

Create a meal as an ethnographic project. Students are asked to create a "food event": plan a meal; select a place where it will be consumed, which may be a home or a restaurant; and invite one or more people to join you. Record your reasons for these decisions and the processes through which you move from planning to preparing this meal and reflecting on this experience. Analyze these in conversation with assigned readings and questions formulated by instructors.

Chapter 4

1. Soundwalk

Provide a map of the university campus to your students. Have students form teams of two or three, and ask them to explore the campus by paying attention to the sounds they encounter. Tell them to write a short description of the sounds on the map. When they come back to the classroom, discuss the sounds encountered. You can show an empty version of the map on the board (using a projector) to identify where the sounds were heard and add them directly as students mention them. If time is limited, collect the maps at the end of the soundwalk, scan them, place them in a PowerPoint presentation, and at the next class, show the students the different sounds that were heard by the different teams. Discuss the similarities and differences between each map.

2. Creating an Original Soundscape

Because this exercise is slightly more complex, I have organized the exercise into a step-by-step process that you might want to adapt to your desired learning outcomes. The idea is to have students create an original soundscape based mainly on their own recordings and on copyright-free sound clips.

– Step 1: Select a nearby work of art, object, or architectural feature.

The visual and the material dimensions will become a jumping-off point to explore the sonic dimension. Often, people relate more easily to the visual than to the sonic, as the former often seems more concrete. The soundscape should be composed in relation with the selected object, the piece of art or the shape; that's how you should find your inspiration. The visual provides a concrete element to help your students start thinking about recording and editing sound. Objects and works of art can be selected on campus.

– Step 2: Record and share sounds.

It is not difficult to learn the basics of sound recording. Many online tutorials show how to record sound, using both amateur and professional equipment. Tell your students that they should not hold back from recording sounds because they do not own a sound recording device. Your students can use any type of equipment such as a smartphone, a basic portable device, or even a camera. Of course, if your students have access to semi-professional or professional equipment, it is worth exploring and trying it out. Many libraries can loan you equipment with an external microphone. I provide my students with very basic training in sound recording. The aim of the exercise is not to produce sound technicians, but to provide hands-on experiences, allowing you to reflect on the recording process and on what you are recording. Questions you want your students to ask themselves while recording sound clips: What is the message you want to convey through your soundscape? What are the different elements that can be included? How can you find the sounds that you want to record? How difficult is it to record one specific sound?

Hopefully, the process of recording sounds will raise your students' awareness of the soundscapes that surround us. Your students should

become attuned to sounds that they never noticed before. This is part
of what I call "the sonic awakening."

Note: In a classroom context, I am extremely rigorous with copyright issues
and I ask my students to use only copyright-free sound recordings,
which are their own recordings or those found in copyright-free
archives such as freesound.org. I also ask students to post at least 10
sound clips on a Soundcloud page that I create for the group. They
can use the sounds recorded by their peers in their own compositions.
Sharing sounds allows the students to discuss and compare sounds with
one another. Some also find inspiration in listening to other students'
recorded clips. At the end of the exercise, if everyone contributed as
requested, we have a pool of close to 200 sounds to work with.

– Step 3: Edit the soundscape.

Ask your students to download the free open-source program Audacity,
which is available online and is compatible with Windows, Mac, and
GNU/Linux. They may also use any other sound/video programs you
have access to (GarageBand, Soundtrack Pro, FL Studio, etc.).

In Audacity, tell them to open a new project and save it in a folder. They
should save all their sound clips in the same folder. Audacity is a
simple program and it follows the same principle as most user-friendly
Microsoft programs. It is often used to create podcasts. Your students
can watch tutorials online.

Ask your students to choose their keynote sounds, defined as those sounds
"which are heard by a particular society continuously or frequently
enough to form a background against which other sounds are
perceived" (Schafer 1994, 272). Silence does not exist. There are always
subtle sounds that fill up the background of a soundscape. The keynote
sound is the first sound clip students should import on their timeline.
It should last the entire time of their soundscape; it should not invade
their composition but should remain audible in the background.

Students need to be careful with timing—the final soundscape
composition should not exceed 2 minutes.

Tell your students to place sound clips on their timeline and experiment
with effects and sound volumes.

Your students should work with headphones but also play their soundscape
on speakers to make sure that the sound is not oversaturated.

When they are done, they can export their soundscape in .wav or .mp3
format.

– Step 4: Present the soundscape.

Have students informally present their soundscape to their peers by showing
a photograph of the piece, object, or architectural feature that influenced

their work as they play their composition. Feedback from the audience is welcome.

Examples produced by third-year undergraduate students at the Royal BC Museum in Victoria can be found at this address: http://learning. royalbcmuseum.bc.ca/playlist/soundscape-composition-anthropology-of-sound-students

– Step 5: Reflect on the process and on the soundscape.

Just as the soundscape is key to conveying an interpretation of visual or material components, writing about the process is key to allowing your students to elaborate on the meanings and sonic symbolism represented in their piece. The exercise of expressing and writing down the reasons why they selected one sound over another, why one sound was amplified and another repeated, for instance, allows them to reflect on their approach and their work in a way that goes beyond the sonic and the object itself. What was their intention in creating a particular piece? Whether or not the piece was successful, their explanation of its rationale allows the listeners to perceive the ways in which they are able to use their hands-on experience to develop an awareness of sound as a significant part of our environment. Through the process of producing the soundscape, the students will certainly realize their potential agency, as social and cultural actors, in transforming our sonic environment (and our perception of it) through our imagination.

Chapter 5

1. Sitting and Walking Interviews

The following exercise helps students to reflect on the difference between "sitting" and "walking" interviews, and to understand the spatial, performative, and embodied dimensions of walking. It consists of two main parts. At first, a student will describe her or his experiences of being a student to another class member while sitting in the classroom. Following this conversation, the speaker will become a "guide" and show her or his exercise partner places on campus that speak to those experiences. These are the instructions for the exercise; two possible formats are suggested for the walking section.

– Step 1.

Find a person in your class to work with. Decide who will be the speaker or guide, and who the listener or audience. Speaker, describe to your partner your experience of attending school here and some of the key places on campus: What is it like for you to be a student? What are some advantages and challenges of attending school here?

What are some of your experiences of this campus, university, or college? Which places are conducive to health, happiness, justice, knowledge, or positive social relations? Which are negative spaces for you?

– Step 2.

Speaker, you will now become a guide. Take your partner for a campus walk; choose one of the two walking tour formats below.

Format A

Choose three "stations" based on the criteria below, and guide your companion through each, explaining why you chose them:
  –A place that reminds you of someone or a particular event.
  –A place that embodies a problem: something you would like to change about the university, about the city you inhabit, or about being a student.
  –A place where you go to find help, inspiration, or support.

Format B

Guide your companion through these three "stations":
  –If you were the Big Bad Wolf, [1] which buildings or sites would you like to "huff and puff and blow down," and why?
  –If you were Little Red Riding Hood, where would your grandmother live, and why there?
  –If you were Jack, where would you plant your magic beans, and where would you want the magic bean vine to take you?

– Step 3.

Return to the classroom, discuss the exercise, and select one of the stations to describe to others. What are some of the differences between sharing your experiences while sitting in the classroom and while walking to and showing the actual locations on campus?

2. Booklets

Create booklets using folded, stapled paper. Give a blank booklet to all the students in your class. (This exercise could be done in a classroom, or could be completed over several weeks by students visiting and documenting city places of their choice.) Ask the students to do the following:

1. On the first page of this booklet, describe a public space (as defined by you) that could be the first station of a possible walking tour, and write a commentary on this location. What would you like other people to notice or learn about this site? What is significant, interesting, or concerning about this place, or about the events/stories associated with it?

2. Leave the other pages of the booklet blank.

3. When the students have completed the first page of the booklet, ask them to pass it along to another person. Ask each student to read the booklet they received, and to add another "station" on the next page. Repeat this process until you have at least four or five different sites and commentaries in each booklet.

3. Mapping

As a class, you can experiment with mapping, remapping, and unmapping your community or one of its areas, by having students annotate, modify, or cut an existing map. (This exercise works well with the free tourist maps you may find at visitor centers and hotels.) If you start by photocopying the "official" map onto one or more transparency sheets, you can overlay several versions of the same map, and compare them at the end of the exercise. These are some questions to start with:

– How could you remap the city and its most significant public spaces? Would you rename some of its plazas, streets, or parks, and if so, why?

– Which stories, people, events, names, languages, and perspectives have been erased from or ignored by "official" maps?

– Draw and annotate your map to add an imaginary, "utopian" layer to your city or neighborhood. What are the places, people, and resources that are not present but that you wish were there? Which locations would you like to erase from the map?

Chapter 6

1. Performance of Ethnography

Divide students into small groups of three or four, and have them designate one student as the ethnographer and the others as interlocutors. Ask the ethnographer to conduct a short, five-minute interview with the interlocutors on a topic of his or her choice. Subsequently, have the ethnographer and interlocutors co-write a short fictional dramatic dialogue or dramatic scenario based on the interview that could later be adapted for the stage.

2. Performance as Ethnography Exercise

Divide students into small groups of three or four, and have them designate one student as the ethnographer and the others as interlocutors. Ask the ethnographer to formulate a research question, and then address it by collaboratively developing a short performance. The students can carry out the exercise by brainstorming how to stage the performance in terms of the spoken text, choreography, stage design, lighting, costumes, and props, or—space and resources permitting—by rehearsing and presenting a short performance in front of class. After students complete Exercises 1 and 2, engage them in a discussion about the advantages and disadvantages of the two approaches.

References

Madden, Matt. 2005. *99 Ways to Tell a Story: Exercises in Style.* New York: Chamberlain Bros.

Schafer, R. Murray. [1977] 1994. *The Soundscape: Our Sonic Environment and the Tuning of the World.* Rochester, N Y: Destiny Books.

Williams, Raymond. 1985. *Keywords: A Vocabulary of Culture and Society.* New York: Oxford University Press.

Note

1 The Big Bad Wolf refers to the fairy tale of the three pigs who constructed straw, wood, and brick houses to protect themselves from a hungry wolf. Little Red Riding Hood, the character of another popular fairy tale, went to visit her sick grandmother only to find out that a wolf had eaten her. Jack, another fairy tale protagonist, planted magic beans that grew very rapidly and took him to a world inhabited by a scary giant.

INDEX